Upstream

Upstream

SELECTED ESSAYS

Mary Oliver

PENGUIN PRESS
New York
2016

PENGUIN PRESS
An imprint of Penguin Random House LLC
375 Hudson Street
New York, New York 10014
penguin.com

Library of Congress Cataloging-in-Publication Data

Names: Oliver, Mary, 1935- author.
Title: Upstream: Select Essays / Mary Oliver.
Description: New York: PENGUIN PRESS, 2016.
Identifiers: LCCN 2016043612 (print) | LCCN 2016050445 (ebook) | ISBN
9781594206702 (hardcover) | ISBN 9780698405622 (ebook)
Classification: LCC PS3565.L5 A6 2016 (print) | LCC PS3565.L5 (ebook) |
DDC 813/.54—dc23
LC record available at https://lccn.loc.gov/2016043612

Printed in the United States of America
9   10

DESIGNED BY AMANDA DEWEY

For Anne Taylor

Contents

Section Four

Section Five

. . . in solitude, or in that deserted state when we are surrounded by human beings and yet they sympathise not with us, we love the flowers, the grass and the waters and the sky. In the motion of the very leaves of spring in the blue air there is then found a secret correspondence with our heart.

Shelley, *On Love*

SECTION ONE

Upstream

One tree is like another tree, but not too much. One tulip is like the next tulip, but not altogether. More or less like people—a general outline, then the stunning individual strokes. Hello Tom, hello Andy. Hello Archibald Violet, and Clarissa Bluebell. Hello Lilian Willow, and Noah, the oak tree I have hugged and kissed every first day of spring for the last thirty years. And in reply its thousands of leaves tremble! What a life is ours! *Doesn't anybody in the world anymore want to get up in the*

middle of the night and
sing?

In the beginning I was so young and such a stranger to myself I hardly existed. I had to go out into the world and see it and hear it and react to it, before I knew at all who I was, what I was, what I wanted to be. Wordsworth studied himself and found the subject astonishing. Actually what he studied was his relationship to the harmonies and also the discords of the natural world. That's what created the excitement.

I walk, all day, across the heaven-verging field.

And whoever thinks these are worthy, breathy words I am writing down is kind. Writing is neither vibrant life nor docile artifact but a text that would put all its money on the hope of suggestion. *Come with me into the field of sunflowers* is a better line than anything you will find here, and the sunflowers themselves far more wonderful than any words about them.

I walked, all one spring day, upstream, sometimes in the midst of the ripples, sometimes along the shore. My company were violets, Dutchman's-breeches, spring beauties, trilliums, bloodroot, ferns rising so curled one could feel the upward push of the delicate hairs upon their bodies. My parents were downstream, not far away, then farther away because I was walking the wrong way, upstream instead of downstream. Finally I was advertised on the hotline of help, and yet there I was, slopping along happily in the stream's coolness. So maybe it was the right way after all. If this was lost, let us all be lost always. The beech leaves were just slipping their copper coats; pale green and quivering they arrived into the year. My heart opened, and opened again. The water pushed against my effort, then its glassy permission to step ahead touched my ankles. The sense of going toward the source.

I do not think that I ever, in fact, returned home.

Do you think there is anything not attached by its unbreakable cord to everything else? Plant your peas and your corn in the field when the moon is full, or risk failure. This has been understood since planting began. The attention of the seed to the draw of the moon is, I suppose, measurable, like the tilt of the planet. Or, maybe not— maybe you have to add some immeasurable ingredient made of the hour, the singular field, the hand of the sower.

It lives in my imagination strongly that the black oak is pleased to be a black oak. I mean all of them, but in particular one tree that leads me into Blackwater, that is as shapely as a flower, that I have often hugged and put my lips to. Maybe it is a hundred years old. And who knows what it dreamed of in the first springs of its life, escaping the cottontail's teeth and everything dangerous else. Who knows when supreme patience took hold, and the wind's wandering among its leaves was enough of motion, of travel.

Little by little I waded from the region of coltsfoot to the spring beauties. From there to the trilliums. From there to the bloodroot. Then the dark ferns. Then the wild music of the waterthrush.

When the chesty, fierce-furred bear becomes sick he travels the mountainsides and the fields, searching for certain grasses, flowers, leaves and herbs, that hold within themselves the power of healing. He eats, he grows stronger. Could you, oh clever one, do this? Do you know anything about where you live, what it offers? Have you ever said, "Sir Bear, teach me. I am a customer of death coming, and would give you a pot of honey and my house on the western hills to know what you know."

———

After the waterthrush there was only silence.

Understand from the first this certainty. Butterflies don't write books, neither do lilies or violets. Which doesn't mean they don't know, in their own way, what they are. That they don't know they are alive—that they don't *feel*, that action upon which all consciousness sits, lightly or heavily. Humility is the prize of the leaf-world. Vainglory is the bane of us, the humans.

Sometimes the desire to be lost again, as long ago, comes over me like a vapor. With growth into adulthood, responsibilities claimed me, so many heavy coats. I didn't choose them, I don't fault them, but it took time to reject them. Now in the spring I kneel, I put my face into the packets of violets, the dampness, the freshness, the sense of ever-ness. Something is wrong, I know it, if I don't keep my attention on eternity. May I be the tiniest nail in the house of the universe, tiny but useful. May I stay forever in the stream. May I look down upon the windflower and the bull thistle and the coreopsis with the greatest respect.

Teach the children. We don't matter so much, but the children do. Show them daisies and the pale hepatica. Teach them the taste of sassafras and wintergreen. The lives of the blue sailors, mallow, sunbursts, the moccasin flowers. And the frisky ones—inkberry, lamb's-quarters, blueberries. And the aromatic ones—rosemary, oregano. Give them peppermint to put in their pockets as they go to school. Give them the fields and the woods and the possibility of the world salvaged from the lords of profit. Stand them in the stream, head them upstream, rejoice as they learn to love this green space they live in, its sticks and leaves and then the silent, beautiful blossoms.

Attention is the beginning of devotion.

My Friend Walt Whitman

In Ohio, in the 1950s, I had a few friends who kept me sane, alert, and loyal to my own best and wildest inclinations. My town was no more or less congenial to the fact of poetry than any other small town in America—I make no special case of a solitary childhood. Estrangement from the mainstream of that time and place was an unavoidable precondition, no doubt, to the life I was choosing from among all the lives possible to me.

I never met any of my friends, of course, in a usual way—they were strangers, and lived only in their writings. But if they were only shadow-companions, still they were constant, and powerful, and amazing. That is, they said amazing things, and for me it changed the world.

This hour I tell things in confidence,
I might not tell everybody but I will tell you.

Whitman was the brother I did not have. I did have
an uncle, whom I loved, but he killed himself one rainy
fall day; Whitman remained, perhaps more avuncular
for the loss of the other. He was the gypsy boy my sister
and I went off with into the far fields beyond the town,
with our pony, to gather strawberries. The boy from Ro-
mania moved away; Whitman shone on in the twilight
of my room, which was growing busy with books, and
notebooks, and muddy boots, and my grandfather's old
Underwood typewriter.

> My voice goes after what my eyes cannot reach,
> With the twirl of my tongue I encompass worlds
> and volumes of worlds.

When the high school I went to experienced a crisis
of delinquent student behavior, my response was to start
out for school every morning but to turn most mornings
into the woods instead, with a knapsack of books. Always Whitman's was among them. My truancy was extreme, and my parents were warned that I might not
graduate. For whatever reason, they let me continue to
go my own way. It was an odd blessing, but a blessing all
the same. Down by the creek, or in the wide pastures I
could still find on the other side of the deep woods, I

spent my time with my friend: my brother, my uncle, my best teacher.

> The moth and the fisheggs are in their place,
> The suns I see and the suns I cannot see are in
>   their place,
> The palpable is in its place and the impalpable is
>   in its place.

Thus Whitman's poems stood before me like a model of delivery when I began to write poems myself: I mean the oceanic power and rumble that travels through a Whitman poem—the incantatory syntax, the boundless affirmation. In those years, truth was elusive—as was my own faith that I could recognize and contain it. Whitman kept me from the swamps of a worse uncertainty, and I lived many hours within the lit circle of his certainty, and his bravado. *Unscrew the locks from the doors! Unscrew the doors themselves from their jambs!* And there was the passion which he invested in the poems. The metaphysical curiosity! The oracular tenderness with which he viewed the world—its roughness, its differences, the stars, the spider—nothing was outside the range of his interest. I reveled in the specificity of his words. And his faith—that kept my spirit buoyant surely, though his faith was without a name that I ever heard of. *Do you guess I have some intricate purpose? Well I have . . . for the April rain has, and the mica on the side of a rock has.*

But first and foremost, I learned from Whitman that the poem is a temple—or a green field—a place to enter, and in which to feel. Only in a secondary way is it an intellectual thing—an artifact, a moment of seemly and robust wordiness—wonderful as that part of it is. I learned that the poem was made not just to exist, but to speak—to be company. It was everything that was needed, when everything was needed. I remember the delicate, rumpled way into the woods, and the weight of the books in my pack. I remember the rambling, and the loafing—the wonderful days when, with Whitman, *I tucked my trowser-ends in my boots and went and had a good time.*

Staying Alive

We are walking along the path, my dog and I, in the blue half-light. My dog, no longer young, steps carefully on the icy path, until he catches the scent of the fox. This morning the fox runs out onto the frozen pond, and my dog follows. I stand and watch them. The ice prevents either animal from getting a good toe-grip, so they move with the bighearted and curvaceous motions of running, but in slow motion. All the way across they stay the same distance apart—the fox can go no faster, neither can my long-legged old dog, who will ache from this for a week. The scene is original and pretty as a dream. But I am wide awake. Then the fox vanishes among the yellow weeds on the far side of the pond, and my dog comes back, panting.

———

I believe everything has a soul.

Adults can change their circumstances; children cannot. Children are powerless, and in difficult situations they are the victims of every sorrow and mischance and rage around them, for children feel all of these things but without any of the ability that adults have to change them. Whatever can take a child beyond such circumstances, therefore, is an alleviation and a blessing.

I quickly found for myself two such blessings—the natural world, and the world of writing: literature. These were the gates through which I vanished from a difficult place.

In the first of these—the natural world—I felt at ease; nature was full of beauty and interest and mystery, also good and bad luck, but never misuse. The second world—the world of literature—offered me, besides the pleasures of form, the sustentation of empathy (the first step of what Keats called negative capability) and I ran for it. I relaxed in it. I stood willingly and gladly in the characters of everything—other people, trees, clouds. And this is what I learned: that the world's *otherness* is antidote to confusion, that standing *within* this otherness—the beauty and the mystery of the world, out in the fields or deep inside books—can re-dignify the worst-stung heart.

The thin red foxes would come together in the last weeks of winter. Then, their tracks in the snow were not of one animal but of two, where in the night they had gone running together. Neither were they the tracks of hunting animals, which run a straight if tacking line. These would sweep and glide, and stop to tussle. Behold a kicking up of snow, a heeling down, a spraying up of the sand beneath. Sometimes also I would hear them, in the distance—a yapping, a summons to hard and cold delight.

I learned to build bookshelves and brought books to my room, gathering them around me thickly. I read by day and into the night. I thought about perfectibility, and deism, and adjectives, and clouds, and the foxes. I locked my door, from the inside, and leaped from the roof and went to the woods, by day or darkness.

When the young are born, the dog foxhunts and leaves what he has caught at the den entrance. In the darkness below, under snags and roots of trees, or clumps of wild roses whose roots are as thick and long as ship ropes, the vixen stays with the young foxes. They press against her body and nurse. They are safe.

Once I put my face against the body of our cat as she lay with her kittens, and she did not seem to mind. So I pursed my lips against that full moon, and I tasted the rich river of her body.

I read my books with diligence, and mounting skill, and gathering certainty. I read the way a person might swim, to save his or her life. I wrote that way too.

After a few weeks the young foxes play about the den. They are dark and woolly. They chew bones and sticks, and each other. They growl. They play with feathers. They fight over food, and the strongest eats more and more often than the weakest. They have neither mercy nor pity. They have one responsibility—to stay alive, if they can, and be foxes. They grow powerful, and thin, more and more toothy, and more and more alert.

A summer day—I was twelve or thirteen—at my cousins' house, in the country. They had a fox, collared and on a chain, in a little yard beside the house. All afternoon all afternoon all afternoon it kept—

Once I saw a fox, in an acre of cranberries, leaping and pouncing, leaping and pouncing, leaping and falling back, its forelegs merrily slapping the air as it tried to tap a yellow butterfly with its thin black forefeet, the butterfly fluttering just out of reach all across the deep green gloss and plush of the sweet-smelling bog.

—it kept running back and forth, trembling and chattering.

Once my father took me ice-skating, then forgot me, and went home. He was of course reminded that I had been with him, and sent back, but this was hours later. I had been found wandering over the ice and taken to the home of a kind, young woman, who knew my family slightly; she had phoned them to say where I was.

When my father came through the door, I thought— never had I seen so handsome a man; he talked, he laughed, his movements were smooth and easy, his blue eyes were clear. He had simply, he said, forgotten that

I existed. One could see—I can see even now, in memory—what an alleviation, what a lifting from burden he had felt in those few hours. It lay on him, that freedom, like an aura. Then I put on my coat, and we got into the car, and he sat back in the awful prison of himself, the old veils covered his eyes, and he did not say another word.

I did not think of language as the means to self-description. I thought of it as the door—a thousand opening doors!—past myself. I thought of it as the means to notice, to contemplate, to praise, and, *thus*, to come into power.

In books: truth, and daring, passion of all sorts. Clear and sweet and savory emotion did not run in a rippling stream in my personal world—more pity to it! But in stories and poems I found passion unfettered, and healthy. Not that such feelings were always or even commonly found in their clearest, most delectable states in all the books I read. Not at all! I saw what skill was needed, and persistence—how one must bend one's spine, like a hoop, over the page—the long labor. I saw the difference between doing nothing, or doing a little, and the redemptive act of true effort. Reading, then writing, then desiring to write well, shaped in me that most joyful of circumstances—a passion for work.

Deep in the woods, I tried walking on all fours. I did it for an hour or so, through thickets, across a field, down to a cranberry bog. I don't think anyone saw me! At the end, I was exhausted and sore, but I had seen the world from the level of the grasses, the first bursting growth of trees, declivities, lumps, slopes, rivulets, gashes, open spaces. I was some slow old fox, wandering, breathing, hitching along, lying down finally at the edge of the bog, under the swirling rickrack of the trees.

You must not ever stop being whimsical.

And you must not, ever, give anyone else the responsibility for your life.

I don't mean it's easy or assured; there are the stubborn stumps of shame, grief that remains unsolvable after all the years, a bag of stones that goes with one wherever one goes and however the hour may call for dancing and for light feet. But there is, also, the summoning world, the admirable energies of the world, better than anger, better than bitterness and, because more interesting, more alleviating. And there is the thing that one does, the needle one plies, the work, and within that work a chance to take thoughts that are hot and formless and to place them slowly and with meticulous effort into some shapely heat-retaining form, even as the gods, or nature, or the soundless wheels of time have made forms all across the soft, curved universe—that is to say, having chosen to claim my life, I have made for myself, out of work and love, a handsome life.

Form is certainty. All nature knows this, and we have no greater adviser. Clouds have forms, porous and shapeshifting, bumptious, fleecy. They are what clouds need to be, to be clouds. See a flock of them come, on the sled of the wind, all kneeling above the blue sea. And in the blue water, see the dolphin built to leap, the sea mouse skittering; see the ropy kelp with its air-filled bladders tugging it upward; see the albatross floating day after day on its three-jointed wings. Each form sets a tone, enables a destiny, strikes a note in the universe unlike any other. How can we ever stop looking? How can we ever turn away?

So, it comes first: the world. Then, literature. And then, what one pencil moving over a thousand miles of paper can (perhaps, sometimes) do.

The fox beside the icy pond had been feeding on an old frozen raccoon, a bad heap, bones and tallow and skin, but better than nothing. For weeks, on my early walk along this path, I saw the fox as he dipped into the dark dish of the frozen body, rasping and tearing.

And now my old dog is dead, and another I had after him, and my parents are dead, and that first world, that old house, is sold and lost, and the books I gathered there lost, or sold—but more books bought, and in another place, board by board and stone by stone, like a house, a true life built, and all because I was steadfast about one or two things: loving foxes, and poems, the blank piece of paper, and my own energy—and mostly the shimmering shoulders of the world that shrug carelessly over the fate of any individual that they may, the better, keep the Niles and the Amazons flowing.

And that I did not give to anyone the responsibility for my life. It is mine. I made it. And can do what I want to with it. Live it. Give it back, someday, without bitterness, to the wild and weedy dunes.

The fox is sitting on a sandy rise, it is looking at me. It yawns, the pickets of its teeth glitter. It scratches under its jaw, rises, and in slow, haunchy nonchalance leaps over the slopes of sand, then down a path, walking, then trotting; then it sprints into the shadows under the trees, as if into water, and is gone.

Of Power and Time

It is a silver morning like any other. I am at my desk.
Then the phone rings, or someone raps at the door. I am
deep in the machinery of my wits. Reluctantly I rise, I
answer the phone or I open the door. And the thought
which I had in hand, or almost in hand, is gone.

Creative work needs solitude. It needs concentration,
without interruptions. It needs the whole sky to fly in,
and no eye watching until it comes to that certainty
which it aspires to, but does not necessarily have at once.
Privacy, then. A place apart—to pace, to chew pencils, to
scribble and erase and scribble again.

But just as often, if not more often, the interruption
comes not from another but from the self itself, or some
other self within the self, that whistles and pounds upon
the door panels and tosses itself, splashing, into the pond
of meditation. And what does it have to say? That you

must phone the dentist, that you are out of mustard, that your uncle Stanley's birthday is two weeks hence. You react, of course. Then you return to your work, only to find that the imps of idea have fled back into the mist.

It is this internal force—this intimate interrupter—whose tracks I would follow. The world sheds, in the energetic way of an open and communal place, its many greetings, as a world should. What quarrel can there be with that? But that the self can interrupt the self—and does—is a darker and more curious matter.

I am, myself, three selves at least. To begin with, there is the child I was. Certainly I am not that child anymore! Yet, distantly, or sometimes not so distantly, I can hear that child's voice—I can feel its hope, or its distress. It has not vanished. Powerful, egotistical, insinuating—its presence rises, in memory, or from the steamy river of dreams. It is not gone, not by a long shot. It is with me in the present hour. It will be with me in the grave.

And there is the attentive, social self. This is the smiler and the doorkeeper. This is the portion that winds the clock, that steers through the dailiness of life, that keeps in mind appointments that must be made, and then met. It is fettered to a thousand notions of obligation. It moves across the hours of the day as though the movement itself were the whole task. Whether it gathers as it goes some branch of wisdom or delight, or nothing at all, is a matter with which it is hardly concerned. What this self hears night and day, what it loves beyond all other songs, is the endless springing forward of the clock, those measures strict and vivacious, and full of certainty.

The clock! That twelve-figured moon skull, that white spider belly! How serenely the hands move with their fili-gree pointers, and how steadily! Twelve hours, and twelve hours, and begin again! Eat, speak, sleep, cross a street, wash a dish! The clock is still ticking. All its vistas are just so broad—are *regular*. (Notice that word.) Every day, twelve little bins in which to order disorderly life, and even more disorderly thought. The town's clock cries out, and the face on every wrist hums or shines; the world keeps pace with itself. Another day is passing, a regular and *ordinary* day. (Notice that word also.)

Say you have bought a ticket on an airplane and you in-tend to fly from New York to San Francisco. What do you ask of the pilot when you climb aboard and take your seat next to the little window, which you cannot open but through which you see the dizzying heights to which you are lifted from the secure and friendly earth?

Most assuredly you want the pilot to be his regular and ordinary self. You want him to approach and undertake his work with no more than a calm pleasure. You want nothing fancy, nothing new. You ask him to do, routinely, what he knows how to do—fly an airplane. You hope he will not daydream. You hope he will not drift into some interesting meander of thought. You want this flight to be ordinary, not extraordinary. So, too, with the surgeon, and the ambulance driver, and the captain of the ship. Let all of them work, as ordinarily they do, in confident familiarity with whatever the work requires, and no more. Their ordinariness is the surety of the world. Their ordinariness makes the world go round.

I, too, live in this ordinary world. I was born into it. Indeed, most of my education was intended to make me feel comfortable within it. Why that enterprise failed is another story. Such failures happen, and then, like all things, are turned to the world's benefit, for the world has a need of dreamers as well as shoemakers. (Not that it is so simple, in fact—for what shoemaker does not occasionally thump his thumb when his thoughts have, as we would say, "wandered"? And when the old animal body clamors for attention, what daydreamer does not now and again have to step down from the daydream and hurry to market before it closes, or else go hungry?)

And this is also true. In creative work—creative work

of all kinds—those who are the world's working artists are not trying to help the world go around, but forward. Which is something altogether different from the ordinary. Such work does not refute the ordinary. It is, simply, something else. Its labor requires a different outlook—a different set of priorities. Certainly there is within each of us a self that is neither a child, nor a servant of the hours. It is a third self, occasional in some of us, tyrant in others. This self is out of love with the ordinary; it is out of love with time. It has a hunger for eternity.

Intellectual work sometimes, spiritual work certainly, artistic work always—these are forces that fall within its grasp, forces that must travel beyond the realm of the hour and the restraint of the habit. Nor can the actual work be well separated from the entire life. Like the knights of the Middle Ages, there is little the creatively inclined person can do but to prepare himself, body and spirit, for the labor to come—for his adventures are all unknown. In truth, the work itself is the adventure. And no artist could go about this work, or would want to, with less than extraordinary energy and concentration. The extraordinary is what art is about.

Neither is it possible to control, or regulate, the machinery of creativity. One must work with the creative powers—for not to work with is to work against; in art as in spiritual life there is no neutral place. Especially at the beginning, there is a need of discipline as well as solitude and concentration. A writing schedule is a good suggestion to make to young writers, for example. Also, it is enough to tell them. Would one tell them so soon the whole truth, that one must be ready at all hours, and always, that the ideas in their shimmering forms, in spite of all our conscious discipline, will come when they will, and on the swift upheaval of their wings—disorderly; reckless; as unmanageable, sometimes, as passion?

No one yet has made a list of places where the extraordinary may happen and where it may not. Still, there are indications. Among crowds, in drawing rooms, among easements and comforts and pleasures, it is seldom seen. It likes the out-of-doors. It likes the concentrating mind. It likes solitude. It is more likely to stick to the risk-taker than the ticket-taker. It isn't that it would disparage comforts, or the set routines of the world, but that its concern is directed to another place. Its concern is the edge, and the making of a form out of the formlessness that is beyond the edge.

Of this there can be no question—creative work requires a loyalty as complete as the loyalty of water to the force of gravity. A person trudging through the wilderness of creation who does not know this—who does not swallow this—is lost. He who does not crave that roofless place *eternity* should stay at home. Such a person is perfectly worthy, and useful, and even beautiful, but is not an artist. Such a person had better live with timely ambitions and finished work formed for the sparkle of the moment only. Such a person had better go off and fly an airplane.

There is a notion that creative people are absent-minded, reckless, heedless of social customs and obligations. It is, hopefully, true. For they are in another world altogether. It is a world where the third self is governor. Neither is the purity of art the innocence of childhood, if there is such a thing. One's life as a child, with all its emotional rages and ranges, is but grass for the winged horse—it must be chewed well in those savage teeth. There are irreconcilable differences between acknowledging and examining the fabulations of one's past and dressing them up as though they were adult figures, fit for art, which they never will be. The working, concentrating artist is an adult who refuses interruption from himself, who remains absorbed and energized in and by the work—who is thus responsible to the work.

On any morning or afternoon, serious interruptions to work, therefore, are never the inopportune, cheerful, even loving interruptions which come to us from another. Serious interruptions come from the watchful eye we cast upon ourselves. There is the blow that knocks the arrow from its mark! There is the drag we throw over our own intentions. There is the interruption to be feared!

It is six A.M., and I am working. I am absentminded, reckless, heedless of social obligations, etc. It is as it must be. The tire goes flat, the tooth falls out, there will be a hundred meals without mustard. The poem gets written. I have wrestled with the angel and I am stained with light and I have no shame. Neither do I have guilt. My responsibility is not to the ordinary, or the timely. It does not include mustard, or teeth. It does not extend to the lost button, or the beans in the pot. My loyalty is to the inner vision, whenever and howsoever it may arrive. If I have a meeting with you at three o'clock, rejoice if I am late. Rejoice even more if I do not arrive at all.

There is no other way work of artistic worth can be done. And the occasional success, to the striver, is worth everything. The most regretful people on earth are those who felt the call to creative work, who felt their own creative power restive and uprising, and gave to it neither power nor time.

SECTION TWO

Blue Pastures

M. and I steered our wooden boat with the ratcheting motor to the breakwater and a little beyond, threw out the anchor, and baited our hooks. All afternoon we drew in the trembling lines only to find the hooks clean, the bait taken. We put on more bait; we were without instruction and did not know how long it might take to catch something. Later, it was explained that we had been feeding crabs—calicos, probably, or some elated gathering of the greens. As far as fishing went, we used the wrong bait and did not engage it to the hooks properly, we were in the wrong part of the harbor at the wrong time according to the tides, and so on.

We were rather glad. We meant, of course, to catch fish. Nevertheless, the hours passed pleasantly, and we found that we were content to have wrested no leaping form from the water. The fact that we caught nothing became, in fact, part of the pleasing aspect of the day. The water was deep and luminous and ever moving; the sky clean and distant; the mood more suitable for slow, long-limbed thoughts than for taking from even the simplest husk of body its final thimble of breath.

On the other hand, as I walk the beach, I have found fish that were hooked and gaffed somewhere nearby and then not quite drawn into the boat. So, they are mine. Some dissatisfied fisherman once left three pollack lying on the sand. I carried them home without compunction and made judicious use of their sweet and snowy bodies.

But whether one is part of the action or not, fishing is always one of the apparent vitalities here. The sea surrounds us. It surrounds the houses and the two long, occasionally bending streets. It surrounds idle conversation; it surrounds the mind diving down into what it hopes is original thought.

One summer morning, neighbors brought us a black duck that dogs had chased to exhaustion along the beach. She rested, and ate, and dozed on the cold floor of the shower. That summer there was, in our neighborhood, an old tomcat, stray—except that we had gotten into the habit of giving him supper, as well as occasional assistance for his sometimes ghastly wounds. At twilight, he would enter through the kitchen window, eat, wash, nap, and leave. When he entered and found the duck, his lean hips swung with surprise and malice. The duck froze. Then the moment broke: the duck prinked her feathers and slapped away to the shower; the cat went casually through his routine, then leaped back into summer night.

After a few days we carried the duck to the water's edge. She settled on the waves just at the brimming of the tide and paddled toward her flock, which was at rest near the breakwater. As she moved away we saw, like a black stitch in the water, something moving toward her, then past her, then straight toward us. It was the steep dorsal fin of a shark. How can one understand such timing, what curious sense does it make, in all the happenings of the universe? In it came, close to the shore—an eight- or nine-foot blue shark. Then it turned—something was wrong—it wobbled a little. An eye, as big as a teacup, tipped toward us. The enormous fish hung in the water about the pilings of an unused and dilapidated wharf. Some young men on the shore also saw it, and came, sprinting, with two-by-fours and metal poles. I shouted—why would they hurt it? They paid no attention, and the shark slid away, and then returned again. I shouted a second time—I wrung my hands. The young men stared and grumbled, but they left the wharf. The shark turned and righted itself and boiled away, into the deeper water.

I have seen the bodies of bluefin tuna cleaned (field-dressed, it might be more proper to say), lying on the wharf, waiting for the winches to swing them into the packing plant. Their bodies are the size of horses—seven hundred pounds, eight hundred pounds. More often than not, they are flown to Japan for quick and expensive consumption. Thirty boats may gather off the coast when a bluefin tuna is caught, hoping for more. I saw one only once: in the morning light, in the distance, a golden horse leaping in and out of the waves.

One afternoon I was aboard the whale-watching vessel the *Dolphin* when the big boat steamed past an ocean sunfish, an enormous bulbous affair, its head scarcely distinguishable from the blown body. It floated easily and without a sound; it could have been asleep.

The flounder makes a pretty supper. So does mackerel—a squamation of snow, midnight, and the blue of a stormy sky. The sea clam, when you clean it—when you cut the hoof from the center of the body—flinches back, the pink flesh tightens against the knife. Mussels open without a sound in the steam, but they make a curious sighing sound when you first reach for them on the rocks; perhaps the picker's shadow tells them, the darkness deepening, that their lives are almost over. Nothing tastes so good as the quahog, opened as soon as found, on the flats, in the cold gray light. You cut it loose from the filmy underpinning, slide it onto the tongue. The gulls know how it tastes. They see you do this and turn in midair. With a sudden skirl they drop, tuning their white feathers to swift descent, and stand about you on the sand, and their faces beg.

I have seen bluefish arc and sled across the water, an acre of them, leaping and sliding back under the water, then leaping again, toothy, terrible, lashed by hunger. The fish they are after, a blood-smeared cloud, are driven sometimes in their search for escape onto the very sand. Porgies, perhaps. With chunks missing from their bodies. Half bodies, still leaping.

Striped bass may be eighty pounds, a hundred pounds. I have never seen them in the sea, but I have seen them iced and boxed, or roped to the fishermen's trucks, like the bodies of deer.

Other fish I have seen by chance: cod, the mild whiting. Now and then a dead goosefish on the beach, all of it but the enormous gate of its mouth sagging under the hot sun. Once, a tautog. But, again, I remember that the fisherman in this case, who had hoped for something else, left it on the sand. Once, a sea robin, in a small boy's pail.

Squid occasionally beach themselves, sputtering and rolling in the swash. They take more time to clean than to gather. They taste like chicken, but are richer by far: the taste of five chickens in each tubular body.

Little skates are common. Fishermen dislike them, for they take the bait frequently, and break lines, and use up time, and flop dismally on the sand when released. I have seen fishermen standing on their wide, crenulated wings in order to rip back the hook that dragged the skate forth in the first place. I have seen few fishermen bother to slide them again into the water. They die, and gulls eat them, or the young eagles, when we are fortunate enough to be visited by those great, dark-feathered birds. The strange face of the skate is haunting, and perhaps it haunts the fishermen, too—the human-looking, spit-releasing mouth, and the sudden motion of the thick eyelids as they descend and rise again over the bulging, death-sick eyes. I hope so. Their soft white bellyskin is plucked open in an hour by the rapacious beaks of the gulls. But their cartilage frames waste away slowly. Like small kites they drift on the tides to the upper beach, where they endure a long time.

Merciless, too, are the fishermen to the supple black

dogfish. One finds them, horribly gaffed, or hacked in half, floating out of the water.

But not every fisherman is so knife-quick. Once I was on a boat when a fisherman—a Provincetown man—hauled in an appalling-looking creature: an enormous spider crab, like an angel of desolation, with a domed body a foot across and nearly as high. The long limbs hung limp and were stuck with bits of seaweed and shells, water sluiced out of the vague centrality of its body, between its forelimbs the eyes gazed humbly. The body shell, too, was festooned with fragments of weed and flotsam. The spider crab dresses its body to make a camouflage, reaching back with a limb and daubing itself with whatever materials are lying about. The fisherman sighed and dropped the mess to the bottom of the boat. He knelt, and worked at the hook. "Never take from the sea what you don't use," he said, and stood up, and swung the crab over the gunnel.

And once, too, I gave something back. A friend left us a bluefish. I went down to the edge of the water to clean it. When I had it scaled and slipped the sharp knife into the bellyflesh, it broke open, not from any carelessness of mine but from a fine necessity; the bluefish had been feeding on small fish—sand eels—and its stomach, like a red and tensile purse, was stuffed full. Pieces of sand eels fell out, and among them maybe a half dozen were intact, squirming, unhurt in fact. So quickly, without a moment's warning, does the miraculous swerve and point to us, demanding that we be its willing servant. Swifter than thought my hands scooped them, and plunged them into the cold water, and the film of their siblings' death fell from them. For an instant they throbbed in place, too dazed to understand that they could swim back into life—and then they uncurled, like silver leaves, and flashed away.

The Ponds

Great blue herons, like angels carved by Giacometti, are common. The edges of Clapps Pond or Great Pond are good places to expect them. Occasionally they stay all winter, and I cannot imagine they have an easy time of it. We get little deep snow, for it melts usually in the salt-laden air between us and the mainland. But the ponds freeze, and the marshes. Green herons are also common; every year a pair nests somewhere along the edge of Little Sister Pond.

American egrets come, more often than not in late summer but sometimes earlier. They are a stark white in the intensely green salt marsh at the west end of town. Snowy egrets appear from time to time and prowl the edges of the larger ponds. They hunt with small, silky motions. Their long necks bend a little to the right, a little to the left, while their eyes stare with a mad concentration into the shallow water.

Occasionally a little blue heron, an adult bird, appears in the thick waters of summer, which stir fitfully under the spindles of its legs.

Very early one morning, in late summer, twelve glossy ibis, flashing dark lights of purple and black, strolled the edges of Blackwater Pond.

The center of my landscape is a place called Beech Forest. On this sandy peninsula, the tall beeches with their cool, thick, lime-colored leaves are rare, and their deep, slow lives are recognized in this name-place. Most of these ponds have traditional names. Those without, I have named. Why not? The ponds are uprisings from the water table, shallow and shape-shifting as sand from the dunes blows into them, creating mass here, causing the water to spread in a generally southeast direction, away from the prevailing winter winds which day after day bite and rasp and shovel up the great weight of the sand.

There are pickerel in the ponds. Other fish too—I do not know their names. But I have seen them, on misty mornings, leaping from the pewter water. They are full of bones and I do not know anyone who eats them, though fishermen come in the spring and cast for them. They throw them back, or leave them, dead or alive, on the shores.

The cattails begin to rise in April; toward the end of that month of general upwelling, the stalks are thick and high enough for one to gather the pale green nutritious plaits. Golden club rises too, especially along the edges of Blackwater Pond. The wood ducks are fond of it, and the muskrats.

The frogs begin to sing any time from late March to the second week in April, and they will be noisy and lusty until the end of the month, both in the ponds proper and in the even more shallow marshes and ephemeral pools.

In April, the snapping turtles wake from their long sleep. Sometimes they will float awhile, in a lonely exhaustion, on the surface of the pond, before a vigor fills their powerful bodies again. Once, on the narrow path between Great Pond and Little Sister Pond, my dog lingered, then came along slowly, mouthing something. He spit into my hand an enormous, curved claw. I knew immediately what it was. Some snapping turtles I have seen had heads like the heads of muskrats, and feet the size of a one-year-old child. One, a few years ago, emerged gargantuan and wrinkled among the pond lilies and slouched—its gassy breath coming and going softly, its pouchy throat expanding and contracting—across the muddy shallows. I didn't see it kill anything. Sometimes we get just enough, not too much. Did He who made the lily make you too? I said to it, looking into its unflickering eyes. You know it, the old shag-face answered, and slid back into the pond's black oils.

More young geese and ducks vanish from the water than live to flex their wings. I have found the bones of birds near the dens of foxes, but it is primarily the snapping turtles, watching from beneath the pond surface for the leaflike feet of the young birds to go paddling by, who contrive these disappearances.

Painted turtles are here too, and are common. Also I have seen spotted turtles, in Blackwater Pond, or, at egg-laying time, trudging uphill from the water, or through the damp leaves around the pond.

An aerial view makes sense of the ponds—they are lined up and run from northeast to southwest. As wind and tide moved glacial debris from what is now the outer shore of Truro, and shoaled and packed it into the sweet curve which finishes this cape, an inner depression was formed, and therein lies one of the ponds. As the cape thickened, this depression readjusted, and another "eye" was created, and another pond. Let us send someone back in a few hundred thousand years to see what new ponds may have curled into birth. Unless, of course, the mechanisms have reversed, and there be nothing at all to report but the rising, unopposable sea.

Mallards are here, and black ducks. The mallards stay on the ponds, the black ducks spend time on the bay as well as on fresh water. Blue-winged teal migrate through, and green-winged. I have seen green-winged with young, but the dreamlike blue-winged, with the thin white moon on his face, I see only in the spring and the fall. I saw wood ducks here for the first time in 1977. There are now many nesting pairs.

Ring-necked ducks appear from time to time during migration, and then fly on. Red-breasted mergansers sometimes come over to the ponds from the salt water. In 1985, a shoveler spent a spring morning on Blackwater Pond. Once, in late March 1991, a single hooded merganser appeared on Oak-Head Pond.

Winter ducks on the ponds include bufflehead, many of them, and goldeneyes, and coots, and pied-billed grebes. They all stay well into April.

In May, and you can trust your life to this, loons will fly over the woods and the ponds—the town too—crying, in the early morning.

Both black-backed gulls and herring gulls come to the ponds and splash vigorously, to wash the salt away. Occasionally, in summer, least terns will fly over to Great Pond, and feed there.

The Canada geese—not the flocks that pass without a missed beat overhead, but the nesting pairs and the adolescents that stay throughout the year—are partly wild, partly tame. They are noisy in the air, secretive on the ponds while nesting is going on. Some years there are many young geese, other years there are few. Ask the turtles about it.

One spring I visited every day with a family of young geese, among which there was one whose wings did not develop. The rest of its body grew, the other feathers sprang from their sheaths and lengthened. But the wings remained small and unfeathered. It vanished, one night, to the oblivion of the ill-made, nature's dark throat, try again. The rest of them soon lost their shyness of me, and would climb over my body as I lay beside the pond or wait for me under the pine trees and leap out, a cloud of gray laughers, when I appeared.

By August, the young geese are strong fliers, and the parents take them from the ponds down to the marshes and the shore, where some of them will spend the winter near the salt water. Others fly off, looking for new homelands.

In spring the water of the pond is like blue wool, endlessly tossing. The heavy, cold water has sunk to the black bottom of the pond, and struck by this weight, the bottom water stirs and rises, filling the pond's basins with wild nutrition. It is an annual event, necessary to the appetite of the year. In late spring, the green grasses and reeds break through, and the first foils of the lilies. The wind grows calmer.

I sit at the edge of Great Pond. The morning light strikes the mist and begins to dispel it. On the pond two geese are floating. Beneath them their reflected images glide; between them five goslings are paddling. The goslings have only recently emerged from the grassy hummock of birth and already they are slipping along eagerly on this glassy road. As instantly as they know hunger, they begin to reach out for duckweed, insects, the tips of grasses.

Occasionally I lean forward and gaze into the water. The water of a pond is a mirror of roughness and honesty—it gives back not only my own gaze, but the nimbus of the world trailing into the picture on all sides.

The swallows, singing a little as they fly back and forth across the pond, are flying therefore over my shoulders, and through my hair. A turtle passes slowly across the muddy bottom, touching my cheekbone. If at this moment I heard a clock ticking, would I remember what it was, what it signified?

It is summer now, the geese have grown, the reeds are a bearded green flocculence, full of splinters of light. Across the pond, the purple loosestrife (alien here, but what does that mean—it is recklessly gorgeous) has come into bloom. A fox steps from the woods, its shoulders are bright, its narrow chest is as white as milk. The wild eyes stare at the geese. Daintily it walks to the pond's edge, calmly it drinks. Then the quick head lifts and turns, with a snap, and once again the geese are appraised. Perhaps it looks toward me too. But I am utterly quiet, and half-hidden. The wind is on my side—I am a stone with its feet in the mud. While I watch, the fox lies down beside the purple flowers. For a while it watches the geese, then the lithe body shrugs to a position of comfort among the leaves and the blossoms, and it sleeps.

Sister Turtle

1.

For some years now I have eaten almost no meat.
Though, occasionally, I crave it. It is a continually interesting subject of deep ambiguity. The poet Shelley
believed his body would at last be the total and docile
servant of his intellect if he ate nothing but leaves and
fruit—and I am devoted to Shelley. But I am devoted
to Nature too, and to consider Nature without this
appetite—this other-creature-consuming appetite—is to
look with shut eyes upon the miraculous interchange
that makes things work, that causes one thing to nurture
another, that creates the future out of the past. Still, in
my personal life, I am often stricken with a wish to be
beyond all that. I am burdened with anxiety. Anxiety for
the lamb with his bitter future, anxiety for my own

body, and, not least, anxiety for my own soul. You can fool a lot of yourself but you can't fool the soul. That worrier.

At the edge of the land lie the watery palaces—the ocean shore, the salt marsh, the black-bellied pond. And in them and upon them: clams, mussels, fish of all shapes and sizes, snails, turtles, frogs, eels, crabs, lobsters, worms, all crawling and diving and squirming among the cattails, sea rocks, seaweeds, sea pickles, spartina, lamb's-quarters, sour grass, arrowhead, mallow. Something eats each of these, each of these eats something else. This is our world. The orange mussel has a blue-black fringe along its body, and a heart and a lung, and a stomach. The scallop as it snaps its way through the water, when the east wind blows, gazes around with its dozens of pale blue eyes. The clam, sensing the presence of your hands, or the approach of the iron tine, presses deeper into the sand. Just where does self-awareness begin and end? With the june bug? With the shining, task-ridden ant? With the little cloud of gnats that drifts over the pond? I am one of those who has no trouble imagining the sentient lives of trees, of their leaves in some fashion communicating or of the massy trunks and heavy branches knowing it is I who have come, as I always come, each morning, to walk beneath them, glad to be alive and glad to be there.

All this, as prelude to the turtles.

2.

They come, lumbering, from the many ponds. They dare the dangers of path, dogs, the highway, the accumulating heat that their bodies cannot regulate, or the equally stunning, always possible cold.

Take one, then. She has reached the edge of the road, now she slogs up the impossible hill. When she slides back she rests for a while, then trundles forward again. Emerging wet from the glittering caves of the pond, she travels in a coat of glass and dust. Where the sand clings thickly the mosquitoes, that hover about her like a gray veil, are frustrated. Not about her eyes, though, for as she blinks the sand falls; so at her tough, old face-skin those winged needles hang until their bodies fill, like tiny vials, with her bright blood. Each of the turtles is a female, and gravid, and is looking for a place to dig her nest; each of the mosquitoes is a female also who cannot, without one blood meal, lay her own fertile eggs upon the surface of some quiet pond.

Once, in spring, I saw the rhapsodic prelude to this

enterprise of nest-building: two huge snapping turtles coupling. As they floated on the surface of the pond their occasional motions set them tumbling and heaving over and around again and yet again. The male's front feet gripped the rim of the female's shell as he pressed his massive body tightly against hers. For most of the afternoon they floated so, like a floundered craft—splashing and drifting through the murky water, or hanging motionless among the rising carpets of the pond lilies.

On these first hot days of summer, anywhere along the edges of these ponds or on the slopes of the dunes, I come upon the traveling turtles. I am glad to see them and sorry at the same time—my presence may be a disturbance that sends them back to the ponds before the egg laying has been accomplished, and what help is this to the world? Sometimes they will make the attempt again, sometimes they will not. If not, the eggs will dissolve back into other substances, inside their bodies.

There are other interrupters, far craftier than I. Whether the turtles come through sunlight or, as is more likely, under the moon's cool but sufficient light, raccoons follow. The turtles are scarcely done, scarcely gone, before the raccoons set their noses to the ground, and sniff, and discover, and dig, and devour, with rapacious and happy satisfaction.

And still, every year, there are turtles enough in the ponds.

As there are raccoons enough, sleeping the afternoons away high in the leafy trees.

One April morning I came upon a snapping turtle shell at the shore of Pasture Pond, tugged from the water, I imagine, by these same raccoons. Front to back, it measured more than thirty inches. Later I found leg bones nearby, also claws, and scutes, as they are called—the individual shingles that cover the raw bone of the shell. Perhaps the old giant died during a hard winter, frozen first at the edges and then thoroughly, in some too-shallow cove. Or perhaps it died simply in the amplitude of time itself— turtles, like other reptiles, never stop growing, which makes for interesting imagined phenomena, if one's inclination is to the bizarre. But the usual is news enough. The adult snapping turtle can weigh ninety pounds, is omnivorous, and may live for decades. Or to put it another way, who knows? The shell I found that April morning was larger than any of my field guides indicates is likely, or even possible.

3.

I saw the tracks immediately—they swirled back and forth across the shuffled sand of the path. They seemed the design of indecision, but I am not sure. In three places a little digging had taken place. A false nest? A foot giving a swipe or two of practice motion? A false visual clue for the predator to come?

I leashed my two dogs and looked searchingly until I saw her, at one side of the path, motionless and sand-spattered. Already she was in the nest—or, more likely, leaving it. For she will dig through the sand until she all but vanishes—sometimes until there is nothing visible but the top of her head. Then, when the nesting is done, she thrusts the front part of her body upward so that she is positioned almost vertically, like a big pie pan on edge. Beneath her, as she heaves upward, the sand falls into the cavity of the nest, upon the heaped, round eggs.

She sees me, and does not move. The eyes, though they throw small light, are deeply alive and watchful. If she had to die in this hour and for this enterprise, she would, without hesitation. She would slide from life into death, still with that pin of light in each uncordial eye, intense and as loyal to the pumping of breath as any-thing in this world.

When our eyes meet, what can pass between us? She sees me as a danger, and she is right. If I come any closer, she will dismiss me peacefully if she can by retracting into her shell. But this is difficult; her bulky body will not fit entirely inside the recesses of that bony hut. She retreats, but still her head is outside, and a portion of each leg. She might hiss, or she might not. She might open the mighty beak of her mouth to give warning, and I might stare a moment into the clean, pale, glossy tun-nel of her inner mouth, with its tag of tongue, before that head, that unexpected long neck flashes out—flashes, I say—and strikes me, hand or foot. She is snake-swift and accurate, and can bite cleanly through a stick three inches thick. Many a dog walks lame from such an en-counter. I keep my dogs leashed and walk on. We turn the corner and vanish under the trees. It is five A.M.; for me, the beginning of the day—for her, the end of the long night.

Of appetite—of my own appetite—I recognize this: it flashes up, quicker than thought; it cannot be exiled; it can be held on leash, but only barely. Once, on an October day, as I was crossing a field, a red-tailed hawk rattled up from the ground. In the grass lay a pheasant, its breast already opened, only a little of the red, felt-like meat stripped away. It simply flew into my mind—that the pheasant, thus discovered, was to be *my* dinner! I swear, I felt the sweet prick of luck! Only secondly did I interrupt myself, and glance at the hawk, and walk on. Good for me! But I know how sparkling was the push of my own appetite. I am no fool, no sentimentalist. I know that appetite is one of the gods, with a rough and savage face, but a god all the same.

Teilhard de Chardin says somewhere that man's most agonizing spiritual dilemma is his necessity for food, with its unavoidable attachments to suffering. Who would disagree.

A few years ago I heard a lecture about the Whitney family, especially about Gertrude Vanderbilt Whitney, whose patronage established the museum of that name in New York City. The talk was given by Mrs. Whitney's granddaughter, and she used a fine phrase when speaking of her family—of their sense of "inherited responsibility"—to do, of course, with received wealth and a sense of using it for public good. Ah! Quickly I slipped this phrase from the air and put it into my own pocket!

For it is precisely how I feel, who have inherited not measurable wealth but, as we all do who care for it, that immeasurable fund of thoughts and ideas, from writers and thinkers long gone into the ground—and, inseparable from those wisdoms because *demanded* by them, the responsibility to live thoughtfully and intelligently. To enjoy, to question—never to assume, or trample. Thus the great ones (*my* great ones, who may not be the same as *your* great ones) have taught me—to observe with passion, to think with patience, to live always caringly.

So here I am, walking on down the sandy path, with my wild body, with the inherited devotions of curiosity and respect. The moment is full of such exquisite interest as Fabre or Flaubert would have been utterly alive to. Yes, it is a din of voices that I hear, and they do not all say the same thing. But the fit of thoughtfulness unites them.

Who are they? For me they are Shelley, and Fabre, and Wordsworth—the young Wordsworth—and Barbara Ward, and Blake, and Basho, Maeterlinck and Jastrow, and sweetest Emerson, and Carson, and Aldo Leopold. Forebears, models, spirits whose influence and teachings I am now inseparable from, and forever grateful for. I go nowhere, I arrive nowhere, without them. With them I live my life, with them I enter the event, I mold the meditation, I keep if I can some essence of the hour, even as it slips away. And I do not accomplish this alert and loving confrontation by myself and alone, but through terrifying and continual effort, and with this innumerable, fortifying company, bright as stars in the heaven of my mind.

Were they seed eaters? Were they meat eaters? Not the point. They were dreamers, and imaginers, and declarers; they lived looking and looking and looking, seeing the apparent and beyond the apparent, wondering, allowing for uncertainty, also grace, easygoing here, ferociously unmovable there; they were thoughtful. A few voices, strict and punctilious, like Shelley's, like Thoreau's, cry out: *Change! Change!* But most don't say that; they simply say: Be what you are, of the earth, but a dreamer too. Teilhard de Chardin was not talking about how to escape anguish, but about how to live with it.

4.

I went back, toward evening, and dug in the sand to the depth of nine inches more or less, and found nothing. There, a few unbroken roots told me the turtle's paddle-shaped feet had gone no farther down. There, as I imagine it, she had shifted the angle of her digging. Perhaps she rested first. Then she began again her sweep-shoving, digging a smaller chamber opening from the original, but narrower, a *sanctum*, to the front of the first. When she was done, a short, fleshy tube descended from her body and reached to this chamber, where the expelled eggs piled up rapidly on the nest of sand.

Into this passage I dug, until my fingers felt the first of the eggs—round, slightly soft; then I began to feel more, and I began to remove them. There were twenty-seven, smaller than Ping-Pong balls, which they somewhat resembled. They were not altogether opaque, but cast a slightly yellow interior light. I placed thirteen in my pocket, carefully, and replaced fourteen in the nest, repacked the nest with sand, and swept from the surface all sign of my digging.

I scrambled them. They were a meal. Not too wonderful, not too bad. Rich, substantial. I could not crack the shells, but had to make a knife slit to enter into each bright chamber. The yolks were large, the whites of the egg scant; the little fertility knot, the bud of the new turtle, was no more apparent than it is in a fertile chicken's egg. There was, in the fabric of the eggs scrambled, a sense of fiber, a tactility, as though a sprinkle of cornmeal had been tossed in, and had not quite dissolved. I imagined it as the building material of the shell. The eggs were small enough that thirteen made no greedy portion. I ate them all, with attention, whimsy, devotion, and respect.

The next morning I went back to the path. I wanted

to see how the nest-place was after one sheet of darkness had gone over it. None of the other prowlers—raccoons, that is—had discovered it. By end of summer, under the provisions of good fortune, the hatchlings, fourteen of them, would rise through the sand. Hardly pausing to consider the world that so suddenly appeared around them, they would turn unerringly toward the dark and rich theater of the nearest pond, would hasten to its edge, and dive in.

Now, in the last hot days of June, I see no more turtles on the paths, nor even their curvaceous wandering trails over the dunes. Now the heat brings forth other buddings and advancements. Almost overnight the honey locust trees have let down their many tassels of blossoms, small white flasks filled with the sweetest honey. I gather handfuls and, for a second, hold them against my face. The fringes of paradise: summer on earth. They, too, will nourish me. Last week I ate the eggs of the turtle, like little golden suns; today, the honey locust blossoms, in batter, will make the finest crepes of the most common pancakes. My body, which must be fed, will be well fed. The hawk, in the pale pink evening, went back to the body of the pheasant. The turtle lay a long time on the bottom of the pond, resting. Then she turned, her eyes upon some flickering nearby as, without terror, without sorrow, but in the voracious arms of the first of the earth's gods, she did what she must, she did what all must do. All things are meltable, and replaceable. Not at this moment, but soon enough, we are lambs and we are leaves, and we are stars, and the shining, mysterious pond water itself.

Wherever I've lived my room and soon
the entire house is filled with books;
poems, stories, histories, prayers of
all kinds stand up gracefully or are
heaped on shelves, on the floor, on
the bed. Strangers old and new offering
their words bountifully and thoughtfully,
lifting my heart.

But, wait! I've made a mistake! how
could these makers of so many books
that have given so much to my life—
how could they possibly be strangers?

M.O.

Emerson:
An Introduction

The distinction and particular value of anything, or any person, inevitably must alter according to the time and place from which we take our view. In any new discussion of Emerson, these two weights are upon us. By time, of course, I mean our entrance into the twenty-first century; it has been two hundred years since Emerson's birth in Boston. By place, I mean his delivery from the town of Concord, and all his corporeal existence anywhere. Now he is only within the wider, immeasurable world of our thoughts. He lives nowhere but on the page, and in the attentive mind that leans above that page.

This has some advantage for us, for he is now the Emerson of our choice: he is the man of his own time—his own history—or he is one of the mentors of ours. Each of these possibilities has its attractions, for the man alive was unbelievably sweet and, for all his devotion to reason, wondrously spontaneous. Yet as time's passage has broken him free of all mortal events, we begin to know him more clearly for the labors of his life: the life of his mind. Surely he was looking for something that would abide beyond the Tuesday or the Saturday, beyond even his first powerful or cautionary or lovely effect. "The office of the scholar," he wrote in "The American Scholar," "is to cheer, to raise, and to guide men by showing them facts amidst appearances." The lofty fun of it is that his "appearances" were all merely material and temporal—brick walls, garden walls, ripening pears—while his facts were all of a shifty vapor and an unauthored goodwill—the luminosity of the pears, the musics of birds and the wind, the affirmative staring-out light of the night stars. And his belief that a man's inclination, once awakened to it, would be to turn all the heavy sails of his life to a moral purpose.

The story of his life, as we can best perceive it from its appearances, is as follows. Ralph Waldo Emerson was born in 1803; his father, William Emerson, died in 1811. The family—his mother, two sisters, and five brothers—were poor, devout, and intellectually ambitious. Death's fast or slow lightning was a too-frequent presence. Both girls and one boy died in childhood; Emerson's brothers

William, Edward, and Charles survived only into early manhood. The only remaining brother to live a life of full length was Robert, who was a man of childish mind. Even as the poet Walt Whitman for most of his life took responsibility for his child-minded brother, Eddie, so did Emerson keep watch over this truculent survivor.

Emerson graduated from Harvard College, then divinity school, and in 1829 began preaching at the Second Church (Unitarian) in Boston. In that year also he married the beautiful but frail Ellen Tucker. Her health never improved, and in 1831 she died. Emerson was then twenty-nine years old.

I think it is fair to say that from this point on, the greater energies of his life found their sustenance in the richness and the steadfastness of his inner life. Soon after Ellen Tucker's death he left the pulpit. He had come to believe that the taking of the sacrament was no more, nor was meant to be more, than an act of spiritual remembrance. This disclosure he made to his congregation, who perhaps were grateful for his forthrightness but in all honesty did not wish to keep such a preacher. Soon after, Emerson booked passage to Europe. He traveled slowly across the continent and, finally, to England. He was deeply touched by the magnificence of the past, so apparent in the cities, in their art and architecture. He also made it his business to explore the present.

The list of those with whom he met and talked is amazing: Coleridge, Wordsworth, Walter Savage Landor, and John Stuart Mill among them. His meeting with Thomas Carlyle began a lifelong friendship, their letters going back and forth across the Atlantic until Carlyle died, in 1881.

Emerson returned from Europe and established a manner of living that he would scarcely alter for the rest of his life. He married again, a young woman named Lydia Jackson. In his journals, which he had begun in college and never abandoned, he tore down wall after wall in his search for a style and for ideas that would reach forth and touch both poles: his certainty and his fluidity. He bought a house in the town of Concord, an easy distance from Boston yet a place with its own extraordinary style and whose citizens were farmers, tradesmen, teachers, and the liveliest of utopians. Here, as husband and father, as writer and lecturer, Emerson would live for years his seemingly quiet, seemingly peaceful life.

The best use of literature bends not toward the narrow and the absolute but to the extravagant and the possible. Answers are no part of it; rather, it is the opinions, the rhapsodic persuasions, the engrafted logics, the clues that are to the mind of the reader the possible keys to his own self-quarrels, his own predicament. This is the crux of Emerson, who does not advance straight ahead but wanders to all sides of an issue; who delivers suggestions with a kindly gesture—who opens doors and tells us to look at things for ourselves. The one thing he is adamant about is that we *should* look—we *must* look—for that is the liquor of life, that brooding upon issues, that attention to thought even as we weed the garden or milk the cow.

This policy, if such it might be called, he established at the start. The first book he published was called *Nature*; in it he refers, with equal serenity, to "Nature" and to "nature." We understand clearly that by the first he means "this web of God"—everything that is not the mind uttering such words—yet he sets our lives down among the small-lettered noun as well, as though to burden us equally with the sublime and the common. It is as if the combination—the necessary honoring of both— were the issue of utmost importance. *Nature* is a text that is entirely about divinity and first purposes, a book of manners, almost, but for the inner man. It does not demean by diction or implication the life that we are most apt to call "real," but it presupposes the heart's spiritual awakening as the true work of our lives. That this might take place in as many ways as there are persons alive did not at all disturb Emerson, and that its occurrence was the beginning of paradise here among the temporal fields was one of his few unassailable certainties.

In 1836, at the issue of this initial volume, and in the first years following, he was a man scarcely known to the world. Descended from seven generations of preachers, in conventional terms a failed churchman himself, he held no more important post than his membership in the Concord volunteer Fire Association. If he tried to be at home among the stars, so, too, he strove to be comfortable in his own living room. Mentor to Thoreau and neighbor to Hawthorne, the idiosyncratic Bronson Alcott, the passionate Margaret Fuller, the talkative Ellery Channing, and the excitable Jones Very, he adorned his society with friendliness and participation. His house was often full of friends, and talk. Julian Hawthorne, then a young boy, remembers him sitting in the parlor, "legs crossed, and—such was their flexibility—with one foot hitched behind the other ankle. Leaning forward, elbow on one knee, he faced his guests and held converse." There was an evening when his daughter Ellen called him away to talk to the butcher about mutton. It is reported that he rose mildly to do as he was bid. And there is another story—as he reported it himself in his journal, on a June day: "Now for near five years I have been indulged by the gracious Heaven in my long holiday

in this goodly house of mine, entertaining and entertained by so many worthy and gifted friends, and all this
time poor Nancy Barron, the mad-woman, has been
screaming herself hoarse at the Poorhouse across the
brook and I still hear her whenever I open my window."

Emerson was the leading member of the group we
know as the New England transcendentalists. It is hardly
a proper philosophy; certainly it is not a school of
thought in which all members were in agreement. Impossible such a finding would have been with the various
sensibilities of Concord! For each member, therefore, it
must be reported somewhat differently. For Emerson, it
devolved from Coleridge and German philosophy, from
Swedenborg, no doubt from half a hundred other voices,
as from his religious beliefs and his own appreciation of
the world's more-than-utilitarian beauty. For Emerson,
the value and distinction of transcendentalism was very
much akin to this swerving and rolling away from acute
definition. All the world is taken in through the eye, to
reach the soul, where it becomes *more*, representative of
a realm deeper than appearances: a realm ideal and sublime, the deep stillness *that is*, whose whole proclama-
tion is the silence and the lack of material instance in
which, patiently and radiantly, the universe exists. Emerson would not turn from the world, which was domestic,
and social, and collective, and required action. Neither

would he swerve from that unperturbable inner radiance, mystical, forming no rational word but drenched with passionate and untranslatable song. A man should want to be domestic, steady, moral, politic, reasonable. He should want also to be subsumed, whirled, to know himself as dust in the fingers of the wind. This was his supple, unbreakable faith.

His certainty that a man must live also in this world, enjoined with the similar faith of the other transcendentalists, was no small force in the New England of the 1830s and 1840s, especially in speech and action on behalf of abolition. Slow as he often was to express outrage, Emerson burst forth in his journal thus: "This filthy enactment [of the Fugitive Slave Law] was made in the 19th century, by people who could read and write. I will not obey it, by God." And he did not.

Writing that loses its elegance loses its significance. Moreover, it is no simple matter to be both inspirational and moderate. Emerson's trick—I use the word in no belittling sense—was to fill his essays with "things" at the same time that his subject was conceptual, invisible, no more than a glimmer, but a glimmer of immeasurable sharpness inside the eye. So he attached the common word to the startling idea. "Hitch your wagon to a star," he advised. "The drop is a small ocean." "A foolish consistency is the hobgoblin of little minds." "We live amid surfaces, and the true art of life is to skate well on them." "Sleep lingers all our lifetime about our eyes, as night hovers all day in the boughs of the fir tree." "The soul makes the body." "Prayer is the contemplation of the facts of life from the highest point of view," he says, and suddenly that elite mystical practice seems clearer than ever before, and possible to each of us.

Of course his writing is made up of the nineteenth-century sentence, so nimble with commas. The sparks of his expression move forward softly and reasonably, in their shapely phrases—then they leap. He rests upon the gnomic as a poet will rest upon meter, and comes not to a conclusion but to a pause in which the reader's own impetus, given such a bright shove, takes over. And yet it is not ornamental eloquence, but natural, fecund, ripe, full of seed, and possibility. Even, or especially (it is his specialty, after all), when talking about the utterly unprovable, he sends out good news, as good reports come all day from the mockingbird, or the soft tongues of the Merrimack. The writing is a pleasure to the ear, and thus a tonic to the heart, at the same time that it strikes the mind.

Thus he wrote and lectured, often in Boston and New York but also as far west as Missouri and beyond. He did not especially like travel, or being away from home, but needed the money and trusted the lecturing process as a way for him to develop and polish his essays for eventual publication.

In 1847, Emerson, by then an established writer widely honored on both sides of the Atlantic, returned to England. The audiences for his lectures were large and curious. Crabb Robinson, in his diary of those years, relates first his own response and then the reaction of the writer Harriet Martineau:

> Tuesday, I heard Emerson's first lecture, "On the Laws of Thought;" one of those rhapsodical exercises of mind, like Coleridge's in his "Table Talk," and Carlyle's in his Lectures, which leave a dreamy sense of pleasure, not easy to analyze, or render an account of. . . . I can do no better than tell you what Harriet Martineau says about him, which, I think, admirably describes the character of his mind. "He is a man so *sui generis*, that I do not wonder at his not being apprehended till he is seen. His influence is of a curious sort. There is a vague nobleness and

thorough sweetness about him, which move people to their very depths, without their being able to explain why. The logicians have an incessant triumph over him, but their triumph is of no avail. He conquers minds, as well as hearts, wherever he goes; and without convincing anybody's reason of any one thing, exalts their reason, and makes their minds worth more than they ever were before."

9TH JUNE, 1848.

That we are spirits that have descended into our bodies, of this Emerson was sure. That each man was utterly important and limitless, an "infinitude," of this he was also sure. And it was a faith that leads, as he shows us again and again, not to stasis but to activity, to the creation of the moral person from the indecisive person. Attachment to the Ideal, without participation in the world of men and women, was the business of foxes and flowers, not of men, not of women. This was, for Emerson himself, difficult. Outwardly he was calm, reasonable, patient. All his wildness was in his head—such a good place for it! Yet his certainty that thought, though it might grow most robust in the mind's repose, was sent and meant for participation in the world, never altered, never ebbed. There are, for myself, a hundred reasons why I would find my life—not only my literary, thoughtful life but my emotional, responsive life—impoverished by Emerson's absence, but none is greater than this uncloseting of thought into the world's brilliant, perilous present. I think of him whenever I set to work on something worthy. And there he is also, avuncular and sweet, but firm and corrective, when I am below the mark. What we bring forth, he has taught me as deeply as any writer could, is predictable.

But let him have the last word. In his journal he wrote:

I have confidence in the laws of morals as of botany. I have planted maize in my field every June for seventeen years and I never knew it come up strychnine. My parsley, beet, turnip, carrot, buck-thorn, chestnut, acorn, are as sure. I believe that justice produces justice, and injustice injustice.

The Bright Eyes of Eleonora: Poe's Dream of Recapturing the Impossible

1.

In Poe's stories and poems we hear continually about compulsion, terrors loosed by the powerful upon the weak (or the powerful components of the mind upon the weak components of the mind); we hear about plague, and tortures, and revenge. But none of these elements does more than forward the real subject of Poe's work, which is the anguish of knowing nothing for sure about the construct of the universe, or about the existence of a moral order within it—anything that would clarify its seemingly total and imperial indifference toward individual destiny.

Poe is no different from any of us—we all choke in

such vapors, somewhat, sometimes. A normal life includes the occasional black mood. But most of us have had some real enough experience with certainty, which helps us to sustain ourselves through passages of metaphysical gloom. While Poe had none. Not little, but none.

This lack disordered him. It is not a spiritual lack, but rather a lack of emotional organization, of confidence. And not self-confidence, which is already a complicated asset, but a lack of confidence in the world entire, and its benevolent as well as malevolent possibilities. In the deepest sense, Poe was without confidence in a future that might be different from the past. He was, forever, reliving an inescapable, original woe.

At the same time he was both a powerful constructor of narrative and a perfect acrobat of language. He was also a man of enormous courage. With almost superhuman will he wrote his poems and his stories—I almost want to say *he wrote and rewrote his story and his poem*—trying to solve the unsolvable and move on. But he never moved on. He never solved anything.

2.

His mother, Eliza Poe, an actress, died when Edgar was two years old. She was twenty-four. It was a pitiful finish to a miserable story: Eliza Poe was penniless, consumptive, and abandoned by Edgar's father, whose occasional and itinerant occupation was also acting.

In Richmond, Virginia, where Eliza died, Poe was taken to live with the John Allan family, perhaps by the whim of Frances Allan, who had no children and had witnessed the death of Eliza. The relationship between Poe and John Allan, a successful merchant, was perpetually and mutually difficult. Though he took the family's name, Poe was never legally adopted.

Poe became friends with a woman named Jane Stanard, the mother of a schoolboy friend. She was a strange, closeted, not too steady figure. Even as their friendship deepened, Jane Stanard sickened, was declared insane, and died. Frances Allan also had never been robust. When Poe was twenty years old, and away from home, Frances Allan died. It was a separation without closure, since John Allan chose not to summon Poe home in time for a last meeting before the final and implacable silence of death.

In 1834, when he was twenty-five, Poe married his cousin Virginia Clemm; she was thirteen years old. Does the future seem ensured? Eight years later, while Virginia was singing, blood began to run from her mouth. It was, it is fair to say, consumption. In 1847 Virginia died. She was twenty-five.

Poe had two years to live. With terrifying gusto, he drank his way through them.

In the Free Library of Philadelphia there is a portrait of the actress Eliza Poe. She is at once curiously stiff and visibly animated; her long black hair curls at the ends and frames the wide brow and the enormous dark eyes. The same dark curls, the same large eyes—in fact, a very similar white, low-bodiced dress—appear in another painting, this one in Richmond, of Frances Allan. And Virginia Clemm? She is described as having had a chalky white complexion, and long black hair, and a high, clear brow, and large eyes that grew even larger and ever more luminous during her illness.

To readers of Poe's poems and tales, it is an altogether familiar face:

> The forehead was high, and very pale, and singularly placid; and the once jetty hair fell partially over it, and overshadowed the hollow temples with innumerable ringlets, now of a vivid yellow, and jarring discordantly, in their fantastic character, with the reigning melancholy of the countenance. ("Berenice")*

*All quotations are taken from *The Collected Tales and Poems of Edgar Allan Poe* (New York: Modern Library, 1992).

I examined the contour of the lofty and pale fore-
head—it was faultless—how cold indeed that word
when applied to a majesty so divine!—the skin ri-
valling the purest ivory, the commanding extent
and repose, the gentle prominence of the regions
above the temples; and the raven-black, the glossy,
the luxuriant, and naturally-curling tresses, setting
forth the full force of the Homeric epithet, "hyacin-
thine"! ("Ligeia")

If the faces of Poe's women are often strikingly similar, other characteristics are no less consistent:

Lo! in yon brilliant window-niche
How statue-like I see thee stand. . . .
    ("To Helen")*

So Poe writes of that pale beauty—that Helen, who
is also Lenore in "The Raven" and Eleonora in the story
named for her. And the Lady Madeline in "The Fall of
the House of Usher" comes from the grave "a *lofty* and
enshrouded figure." And Ligeia "came and departed as
a shadow." And her eyes were large—"far larger than
the ordinary eyes of our own race." There is not the

---

*All italics in quotations are mine.

briefest glimpse of Annabel Lee in the rhapsodic, death-soaked poem of that name, yet we know, don't we, what she must have looked like. Pale, dark-haired, with wide and luminous eyes—vivacious in the trembling, fragile way of mayflies. The narrator says of Berenice: "Oh, gorgeous yet fantastic beauty! Oh, sylph amid the shrubberies of Arnheim! Oh, Naiad among its fountains!" Of Eleonora: "like the ephemeron, she had been made perfect in loveliness only to die." Of Ligeia again: she has "the face of the water-nymph, that lives but an hour" and "the beauty of the fabulous Houri of the Turk."

In Poe's stories overall, no focus is so constant as that of the face and, within the face, the look of the eyes. "The *expression* of the eyes of Ligeia!" the narrator cries aloud and, sacrificing the "blue-eyed Lady Rowena," wills the dead, dark-eyed Ligeia to return to him within the vehicle of Rowena's body. When the corpse stirs slowly and opens its eyes, he shrieks—of course it is the end of the story—"these are the full, and the black, and the wild eyes of my lost love."

Nothing, nothing in all the secret and beautiful and peaceful Valley of the Many-Colored Grass, where the narrator is but a boy and loves for the first time—nothing shines so brightly as the eyes of the first-beloved, Eleonora.

3.

Said the poet Robert Frost, "We begin in infancy by establishing correspondence of eyes with eyes."* It is deeply true. It is where the confidence comes from; the child whose gaze is met learns that the world is real, and desirable—that the child himself is real, and cherished. The look in the eyes of Poe's heroines—it is the same intensity, over and over, upon the long string of his many tales. It is the look that, briefly, begins to give such confidence—then fades.

Not in "Ligeia" and "Berenice" and "Eleonora" only, but in other stories too, the eye is a critical feature. In "The Tell-Tale Heart," the narrator murders an old man of whom he is truly fond because of the blue veil that is cast over one eye. "The vulture eye," he calls it.

> Whenever it fell upon me, my blood ran cold, and so by degrees—very gradually—I made up my mind to take the life of the old man, and thus rid myself of the eye for ever.

---

*Robert Frost: Collected Poems, Prose, & Plays (New York: Library of America, 1995), p. 742.

It is a simple case. The eye that does not look back does not acknowledge. To Poe's narrator, it is unbearable.

The eyes of Augustus Bedloe, in "A Tale of the Ragged Mountains," are

> abnormally large, and round like those of a cat. . . .
> In moments of excitement the orbs grew bright to a
> degree almost inconceivable; seeming to emit lumi-
> nous rays, not of a reflected but of an intrinsic lus-
> tre, as does a candle or the sun.

Bedloe, otherwise a corpse-like figure, gains vigor through his daily use of morphine. He is, we understand, a man who is being medically supervised; he has even been hypnotized. He tells his story: one afternoon, in the mountains of Virginia, he breaks through the wall of time and place. "You will say now, of course, that I dreamed; but not so," he says. But his inexorable original fate, in the trivia of this new time and place, the Virginia wilderness, waits for him. He cannot escape it.

In "The Fall of the House of Usher," the gloomy mansion itself takes on the look of a face, with its "vacant and eye-like windows." The same face makes its grim appearance in the poem "The Haunted Palace." In the tale "William Wilson," on the other hand, such play of eye correspondence is significantly lacking; the two William Wilsons of the story are, of course, one person.

Neither does the flash of the eye, luminous or overcast, play a role in "The Pit and the Pendulum."

> At length, with a wild desperation at heart, I quickly unclosed my eyes. My worst thoughts, then, were confirmed. The blackness of eternal night encompassed me.

Underneath its ropes and rats, its tensions and extraordinary machineries, "The Pit and the Pendulum" is the story of the soul struggling with the tortures of an indifferent universe. It is a tale of unmatchable horror—as it is equally a tale of all but unmatchable endurance. In the context of Poe's work as a whole, both the "eternal night" and the narrator's solitude are elements that make of the pit's chamber an even more terrible tableau. In the blackness of the pit there is nothing—and no one. Not even the eye with the blue veil.

4.

It is not hard to recognize Poe's many narrators as a single sensibility, as one character, and to see this character as other than rational. He is a man of nervous temperament; he is capable of great love, loyalty, grief, of "wild excitement" (a recurring phrase); he owns a strange and unfettered imagination. His enterprise is to challenge and dissolve a particular fact or circumstance that represents the natural order of things—specifically, death's irreversibility. He therefore seeks to understand the world in a way that will disprove such circumstance. Discovering a "different" world assumes *experiencing manifestations of that different world.* To begin, then, it is necessary to disassociate from the world as it is ordinarily experienced. And not casually. He must unstring the universe to its farthest planet and star, and restring it in another way.

His posture is transcendentalism, of the nineteenth-century Germanic variety. The possibilities of alchemy, mesmerism, occultism appeal to him. He is no Orpheus, begging an exception and a second chance, but rather— I mean from his own view—a visionary. To change his own fate, he would change our comprehension of the entire world.

The question of madness is always present. The actions of the narrator are often recognizably insane. But the definitions of madness and rationality have been thrown here into the wind; in Poe's stories, such states are uncertainly bordered areas in which, suddenly, ghosts walk. "Men have called me mad; but the question is not yet settled, whether madness is or is not the loftiest intelligence," the narrator says in "Eleonora."

Illness, as well, is a presence, an excuse for clearly inexcusable actions. The narrator in "Berenice" is named Egaeus, a word wondrously close to "aegis," which, in English schools, is a term meaning a note that signifies sickness as an excuse. It is an uncommon term, but Poe, who went to school in England for five years while the Allans were living in London, no doubt knew it.

Upon the wing of such pure or near madness, the effort toward re-visioning goes on. The mind deranged, by alcohol, opium or morphine, or insanity, sees a world differently from the sane and the sober—*but, in fact, it does see a world.* Poe's narrators drink furiously, and when they can get it, they take into their bodies the white powder opium; thus they lean, trembling, against the walls of ordinary perception. And thus, over and over, with "wild excitement," they "swoon" out of this world.

To swoon is not only to pass from consciousness physically; it may also represent a willingness, even an eagerness, to experience unknown parts of life—obscure regions that might lead one toward a re-visioning. One swoons for many reasons and from many causes—from fever, sheer fright, extreme agitation, from exertion or exhaustion. The effects of opium and alcohol alone, in sufficient doses, will also bring on a kind of swooning; one leaves the realm of the rational and the known for that shapeless, unmapped region of "seeming." What is certain in the rational realm is by no means certain in the kingdom of swoon. *And though nothing in that dark kingdom is provable, neither can its nonexistence be proven.* If nothing there is solid to the hand, it is solid enough to the mind, and upon that smallest beginning the need of the mind builds.

Poe's fascination with enclosed space (the brain shape) as pit, maelstrom, catacomb, ballroom (in "Hop-Frog"), and the many chambers and turrets of castles, reaches a curious pitch in a piece called "Philosophy of Furniture." Here Poe describes, in intense and elaborate detail, his "favorite room." The description is obsessional. Here are carpets and curtains in mute and lustrous colors, paintings, furniture, giltwork and fringe, draperies, mirrors, Sèvres vases, candelabra; we are given not only their exact shapes and colors but their precise placement within the room. It is a room where "repose speaks in all." Yet it is not a bedroom—there is no bed here for sleeping on in the ordinary way of well-earned and deep rest. There are two sofas, and upon one, says Poe, the proprietor lies asleep. But it is sleep as Poe most sought and valued it—not for the sake of rest, but for escape. Sleep, too, is a kind of swooning out of this world.

5.

Poe's work is exquisitely and opulently constructed; the narratives have a fascination that is a sure-hold—a quality that, for lack of another word, one might simply call entertainment. They are frightening—but not in the way that Kafka's "The Metamorphosis," for example, or James's "The Turn of the Screw" is frightening. In spite of the extreme and macabre symbolism in Kafka's story, both "The Metamorphosis" and "The Turn of the Screw" take place in a world uncomfortably familiar, and the stories unfold, both of them, in a terrifyingly low-key, unextraordinary way. They are, horribly and unmistakably, descriptions of life as we know it, or *could* easily know it. While Poe's stories are—stories. Full of the hardware of the nightmare—graves, corpses, storms, moldering castles, catacombs—and hovering always at the edge of tension and incredulity, they never fail to thrill as *stories*.

But literature, the best of it, does not aim to be literature. It wants and strives, beyond that artifact part of itself, to be a true part of the composite human record—that is, not words but a reality.

Poe's work opens on this deeper level when we consider what we know about his life. Such consideration is a tricky business. In our own age such investigation and correspondence is, I think, grossly overdone; hardly a literary melancholy these days is explained in any terms but those of personal grievance. But Poe's case is exceptional. Life-grief was his earliest and his deepest life experience. Not to wonder how deeply it shaped his outlook and his work is to miss something sharply sorrowful, and deeply valiant.

But let us consider the matter in yet another way. Poe's inability to incorporate loss and move on was not a response born of his experience alone, but was also an invention, an endlessly repeatable dark adventure created by his exceedingly fertile mind. For Poe, in an artistically kaleidoscopic brilliance, does not write only about his own argument with the universe, but about everyone's argument.

For are we not all, at times, exactly like Poe's narrators—beating upon the confining walls of circumstance, the limits of the universe? In spiritual work, with good luck (or grace), we come to accept life's brevity for ourselves. But the lover that is in each of us—the part of us that *adores* another person—ah! that is another matter.

In the mystery and the energy of loving, we all view time's shadow upon the beloved as wretchedly as any of Poe's narrators. We do not think of it every day, but we never forget it: the beloved shall grow old, or ill, and be taken away finally. No matter how ferociously we fight, how tenderly we love, how bitterly we argue, how pervasively we berate the universe, how cunningly we hide, this is what shall happen. In the wide circles of timelessness, everything material and temporal will fail, including the manifestation of the beloved. In this universe we are given two gifts: the ability to love, and the ability to ask questions. Which are, at the same time, the fires that warm us and the fires that scorch us. This is Poe's real story. As it is ours. And this is why we honor him, why we are fascinated far past the simple narratives. He writes about our own inescapable destiny.

His words and his valor are all he has, and they are

stunning. When in "The Masque of the Red Death" the stranger who is really nothing but an empty cloak enters and slays the Prince, it is Poe and it is ourselves with him who rush forward and batter hopelessly against that in-comprehensibility, with our frail fists, with "the wild courage of despair."

Some Thoughts on Whitman

1.

In *The Varieties of Religious Experience*, William James offers four marks of distinction that are part of a mystical experience. The first of these is that such an experience "defies expression, that no adequate report of its contents can be given in words."*

All poets know such frustration generally; the goal of creative work is ever approachable yet unattainable. But Whitman as he worked on *Leaves of Grass* may have been grappling with a more splendid difficulty than the usual—there is in his work a sense of mystical thickness and push, and a feeling that the inner man was at work

---

*From *The Varieties of Religious Experience*, in *William James: Writings, 1902–1910* (New York: Library of America, 1987). The particular phrases quoted can be found on pp. 343–44.

under some exceptional excitement and compulsion. Whether Whitman had an actual mystical experience or not,* his was a sensibility so passionate, so affirmative and optimistic, that it is fair to speak of him as writing out of a kind of hovering mystical cloud. Clearly his idea of paradise was here—this hour and this place. And yet he was, in his way, just as the mystic is, a man of difference—a man apart.

James's other marks of distinction concerning the mystical experience are as follows, and also feel much in accord with the emanations of *Leaves of Grass*: that mystical states "are illuminations, revelations . . . and as a rule they carry with them a curious sense of authority for after time"; that such a state "cannot be sustained for long"; and that the mystic feels "as if his own will were in abeyance, and indeed sometimes as if he were grasped and held by a superior power."

Whitman published *Leaves of Grass* in 1855, twelve poems and a prologue which unite into a single work. For the rest of his writing life Whitman wrote no other verse but fed it into that ever-expanding book—that is, all the work of his "after life" was refinement, addition, inculcation. Except in the hope of better effect, he took up no new subjects, nor altered the rhapsodic tenor of

*Ibid., p. 357.

his voice, nor denied any effort of catalog, rhetoric, eroticism, nor trimmed his cadence, nor muted his thunder
or his sweetness. His message was clear from the first
and never changed: that a better, richer life is available to us, and with all his force he advocated it both for
the good of each individual soul and for the good of the
universe.

That his methods are endlessly suggestive rather than
demonstrative, and that their main attempt was to move
the reader toward response rather than reflection, is perhaps another clue to the origin of Whitman's power and
purpose, and to the weight of the task. If it is true that
he experienced a mystical state, or even stood in the
singe of powerful mystical suggestion, and James is
right, then he was both blessed and burdened—for he
could make no adequate report of it. He could only summon, suggest, question, call, and plead. And *Leaves of
Grass* is indeed a sermon, a manifesto, a utopian docu-
ment, a social contract, a political statement, an invitation, to each of us, to change. All through the poem we
feel Whitman's persuading force, which is his sincerity;
and we feel what the poem tries continually to be: the
replication of a miracle.

2.

The prose "Preface" that stands before the poems is wide-ranging and pontifical. Emerson lives here in both thought and word; actual phrases taken from Emerson's essays "The American Scholar" and "The Poet" are nailed down as Whitman's own. Whitman claims for his work the physical landscape and spiritual territory of America; in so doing he turns, like Emerson, from the traditions of Europe. He claims also, for the poet, a mental undertaking that is vast and romantic, and a seriousness that is close to divine.

The twelve poems of the 1855 edition of *Leaves of Grass* consist of one huge and gleaming Alp followed by a relaxed undulation of easily surmountable descending foothills. The initial poem, "Song of Myself" (sixty-two pages*), is the longest and the most critical. It is the Alp. If the reader can "stay with" this extended passage, he

---

*The number of pages devoted to this poem in *Walt Whitman: Complete Poetry and Collected Prose* (New York: Library of America, 1982).

has made a passage indeed. The major demands of the
poem are here established, the first and essential lesson
given in the first half-dozen lines:

> I celebrate myself,
> And what I assume you shall assume,
> For every atom belonging to me as good belongs
>   to you.

> I loafe and invite my soul,
> I lean and loafe at my ease . . . observing a spear
>   of summer grass.   (p. 27)

In these lines the great work is begun, and the secret
of success has been given. And what is that great labor?
Out-circling interest, sympathy, empathy, transference of
focus from the self to all else; the merging of the lonely
single self with the wondrous, never-lonely entirety. This
is all. The rest is literature: words, words, words; example, metaphor, narrative, lyricism, sweetness, persuasion,
the stress of rhetoric, the weight of catalog. The detail,
the pace, the elaborations are both necessary and aug-
mentative; this is a long poem and it is not an argument
but a thousand examples, a thousand taps and twirls on
Whitman's primary statement. Brevity would have made

the whole thing ineffectual, for what Whitman is after is felt experience. Experience only, he understands, is the successful persuader.

> *Logic and sermons never convince,*
> *The damp of the night drives deeper into*
> *my soul* (p. 56)

he says, and what would be prolongation or hyperbole in another man's book is part of the earnest and necessary equipage here.

The reader of *Leaves of Grass*, in this first section especially, is a major player, and is invited into this "theater of feeling" tenderly. "Song of Myself" is sprinkled with questions; toward the end of the poem they come thick and fast, their profusion, their slantness, their un-answerability helping the reader to rise out of familiar territory and into this soul-waking and world-shifting experience:

> *Have you reckoned a thousand acres much? Have*
> *   you reckoned the earth much?* (p. 28)
> *What do you think has become of the young and*
> *   old men?* (p. 32)
> *Who need be afraid of the merge?* (p. 33)
> *The souls moving along . . . are they invisible*

while the least atom of the stones is
visible? (p. 34)
Oxen that rattle the yoke or halt in the shade,
what is that you express in your eyes? (p. 37)
What is a man anyhow? What am I? and what
are you? (p. 45)
Shall I pray? Shall I venerate and be
ceremonious? (p. 45)

And on and on. More than sixty questions in all, and not one of them easily answerable.

Nor, indeed, are they presented for answers, but to force open the soul:

Unscrew the locks from the doors!
Unscrew the doors themselves from their
jambs! (p. 50)

"Song of Myself" presents Whitman's invitation in a tone without margins—ecstasy, mysticism, urgency, se-ducements, open arms, and all those questions leave the reader plundered, exalted, and exhausted.

And so, amazingly, begins the long descent. The eleven poems remaining are various in tone and intention. In comparison with the sixty-two pages of "Song of Myself," each is surprisingly brief. In each section the author of "Song of Myself" continues to speak, but more comfortably, less extensively, less urgently, and at an increasing emotional distance from us.

Two of the poems are eleven pages long, another two are seven pages in length, the last seven are all four pages long or less.* If "The Sleepers" is almost palpably caressing, if "There Was a Child Went Forth" is flawlessly tender, if "A Boston Ballad" stands in its place with a surprising theatricality, still none of them measures anywhere near "Song of Myself," with its thunder and its kisses and its implications. So hot is the fire of that poem, so bright its transformative power, that we truly need, and Whitman knew it, each of the slow, descending chords that follow. There is a madness born of too much light, and Whitman was not after madness nor even recklessness, but the tranquility of affinity and function. He was after a joyfulness, a belief in existence in which man's inner light is neither rare nor elite, but godly and common, and acknowledged. For that it was necessary to be rooted, again, in the world.

---

*Poem lengths are taken from the volume previously cited.

3.

One day as I wrestled with that long opening poem, the complaint burst from me: With Whitman it's opera, opera, opera all the time! I shouted, in something very like weariness.

It is true. For long stretches Whitman's tone of summoning and import is unalleviated. But it is necessary to his purpose, which is so densely serious. Neither whimsy nor the detailed and opulent level of fun-terror, as Poe for example employs it, is found in Whitman. Poe understood the usefulness of entertainment and employed it, although he too was dead serious. Whitman did not, nor even the expansions of narrative. In "Song of Myself" and in passages beyond as well are page after page of portrait and instance; each opens in a blink and shuts on another. They are not stories; they are glances, possibilities. They are any of us, almost, in another life, and they expect of the reader a costly exchange; we cannot glide here upon narrative but must imaginatively take on other destinies:

The pure contralto sings in the organ loft,
The carpenter dresses his plank . . . the tongue

of his foreplane whistles its wild ascending
lisp. . . . *(p. 39)*
The bride unrumples her white dress,
the minutehand of the clock moves
slowly. . . . *(p. 41)*
The pilot seizes the king-pin, he heaves down with
a strong arm. . . .
The deacons are ordained with crossed hands at
the altar. . . .
The lunatic is carried at last to the asylum a
confirmed case. . . . *(p. 39)*

All are unforgettable, even, or especially:

. . . the little child that peeped in at the door
and then drew back and was never seen
again. . . . *(p. 78)*

Along with such portraits and moments of quickness
and essence, Whitman turned upon the least detail of the
manifest world such a fussy and diligent attention that
the long lines lay down not so much ethereal as palpable.
These lines with their iambic cadence and their end stops
are like speech, yet not quite. They lack what speech so
readily has—an uncertainty, a modesty, a feeling of attempt toward expression rather than reiterated exacti-

tude. Which is what Whitman has in such abundance: certitude, and a centering clarity of the least object.

Still, for all its intensity, Whitman's work is grammatically reasonable and abides by established rules. Such grammar-stability, compared for example with the syntactical compressions risked by Hopkins, makes a poetic line that is understandable, supple, and reliable. Such reliability assists Whitman's capacity to stay mild, or to flare, as the need may be. His style is made up of many elements but is not complex. The tones are various: vatic, tender, patriotic, journalistic, impassioned, avuncular, sensual. Insistence and excess are not naturally virtues, but Whitman makes them virtues in the service of his purpose.

Certain understandings still slip the search: How does the tender not become mincing? How does authority avoid pomp? How does cadence repeated and repeated summon rather than lull?

Most writing implies a distant, possible, even probable audience of a few or of many. *Leaves of Grass* assumes an intimate audience of one—one who listens closely to the solitary speaker. That is, to each reader the poem reaches out personally. It is mentoring, it is concerned; it is intimate. It contains the voice of the teacher and the preacher too, but it extends beyond their range. "Touch is the miracle," Whitman wrote in one of his workbooks. The words, in the long lines of *Leaves of Grass*, as near as words can be, are a spiritual and a physical touching.

4.

A great loneliness was Whitman's constant companion, his prod, his necessary Other. One sees it everywhere in his personal life, his professional life, his beautifying portrayals of young men, his intense and prolonged references to the body's joy. It is supposed that a writer writes what he knows about and knows well. It is not necessarily so. A writer's subject may just as well, if not more likely, be what the writer longs for and dreams about, in an unquenchable dream, in lush detail and harsh honesty. Thus Whitman: grown man, lonely man. Sexual longing is the high note in the funneled-forth music of easy companionship with carriage drivers, sailors, wharf roughs, loose male energy, electric and swaggering. What else can we say? What else can we know? That it was not a trivial loneliness, or a passing loneliness, or a body loneliness only, but a loneliness near fatal.

> *The sleepers are very beautiful as they lie*
> *unclothed,*

*They flow hand in hand over the whole earth from
    east to west as they lie unclothed. . . .* (p. 115)

The fetch of his breath and the fetch of his ambition
began on the shores of this loneliness. Without it he
might have relaxed back from the endless and fiery work.
He might have let a little moderation into his rhapsody.
Certainly he would not have been the Whitman we mean
when we say the poet, Whitman.

*Darkness you are gentler than my lover . . . his
    flesh was sweaty and panting,
I feel the hot moisture yet that he left me.* (p. 109)

The erotic and the mystical are no strangers: each is
a tempest; each drowns the individual in the yearn and
success of combination; each calls us forth from an ordinary life to a new measure. For Whitman the erotic life
of the body was all that the word "erotic" means, plus
more; it was also its own music, its authority, and its
manner of glazing our surroundings so that it seems we
have been given new sight. James's four marks of distinction concerning mystical experience might apply without
contortion to the erotic life as well. And Whitman, advo-
cating the affirmative life of the body—I want to say the
luster of the body—was at the same time in an alliance

with the power of transformation. Was Whitman a mystic? For myself, I cannot answer the question except to say that surely he was a religious poet in the same sense that Emerson was a religious man, for whom life itself was light. For Emerson, it was light as clear as spring in his own orchard. For Whitman, it was that hot burning, that heaviness of intent, that vertigo, that trembling: that merge.

Eroticism is, both as eroticism exactly and as metaphor, what *Leaves of Grass* advocates: the healthy, heavy, seeded life of the soul. That such advocacy brought him criticism no doubt was disappointing, but he did not change his work. That he was called coarse and rank must have dismayed him, but he did not alter anything. There was no way he could delete or dilute this part of his cosmology. It was central to everything he wanted to say.

> *To be surrounded by beautiful curious breathing*
> *laughing flesh is enough,*
> *To pass among them . . . to touch any one . . . to*
> *rest my arm ever so lightly round his or her*
> *neck for a moment . . . what is this then?*
> *I do not ask any more delight . . . I swim in it as*
> *in a sea. (p. 120)*

5.

What cannot be told can be suggested; such is the theater of *Leaves of Grass*, hugely long, opulent, illustrative, intense, oracular, tender, luxurious. And you must take it to the hilt, you must stay with it almost beyond endurance, for

> *This is the grass that grows wherever the land is*
> *and the water is,*
> *This is the common air that bathes the*
> *globe.* (p. 43)

Of all American poems, the 1855 *Leaves of Grass* is the most probable of effect upon the individual sensibility. It wants no less. We study it as literature, but like all great literature it has a deeper design: it would be a book for men to live by. It is obsessively affirmative. It is foolishly, childishly obsessively affirmative. It offers a way to live, in the religious sense, that is intelligent and emotive and rich, and dependent only on the individual—no politics, no liturgy, no down payment. Just attention, sympathy, empathy. Neither does Whitman speak of hell or damnation; rather, he is parental and coaxing, tender and provocative in his drawing us toward him. Line by line, he amalgamates to the fact. Brawn and spirit, we are built of light, and God is within us. This is the message of his long, honeyed harangue. This is the absolute declaration, and this is the verifying experience of his poem.

> Swift wind! Space! My Soul! Now I know it is
>   true what I guessed at;
> What I guessed when I loafed on the grass,
> What I guessed while I lay alone in my bed . . .
>   and again as I walked the beach under the
>   paling stars of the morning. (p. 59)

Wordsworth's Mountain

1.

There is a rumor of total welcome among the frosts of
the winter morning. Beauty has its purposes, which, all
our lives and at every season, it is our opportunity, and
our joy, to divine. Nothing outside ourselves makes us
desire to do so; the questions, and the striving toward
answers, come from within. The field I am looking at is
perhaps twenty acres altogether, long and broad. The
sun has not yet risen but is sending its first showers
over the mountains, a kind of rehearsal, a slant light
with even a golden cast. I do not exaggerate. The light
touches every blade of frozen grass, which then burns
as a particular as well as part of the general view. The
still-upright weeds have become wands, encased in a

temporary shirt of ice and light. Neither does this first light miss the opportunity of the small pond, or the groups of pine trees. And now: enough of silver, behold the pink, even a vague, unsurpassable flush of pale green. It is the performance of this hour only, the dawning of the day, fresh and ever new. This is to say nothing against afternoons, evenings, or even midnight. Each has its portion of the spectacular. But dawn—dawn is a gift. Much is revealed about a person by his or her passion, or indifference, to this opening of the door of day. No one who loves dawn, and is abroad to see it, could be a stranger to me.

Poe claimed he could hear the night darkness as it poured, in the evening, into the world. I remember this now and think, reversing the hour but not the idea, that I will hear some sound of the morning as it settles upward. What I hear, though, is no such sprawling and powerful anthem, as it would have to be, but the rustling of a flock of snow buntings, high and wild in the cold air, like seeds, rushing toward me, and then away. Seeds that sing. I see, on this morning, nothing else, or nothing else moving. Fox tracks are ahead of mine, dimpling the frost, but the fox is nowhere in view.

2.

When I was a child, living in a small town surrounded by woods and a winding creek—woods more pastoral than truly wild—my great pleasure, and my secret, was to fashion for myself a number of little houses. They were huts really, made of sticks and grass, maybe a small heap of fresh leaves inside. There was never a closure but always an open doorway, and I would sit just inside, looking out into the world. Such architectures were the capsules of safety, and freedom as well, open to the wind, made of grass and smelling like leaves and flowers. I was lucky, no one ever found any of my houses, or harmed them. They fell apart of the weather, an event that caused me no grief; I moved on to another place of leaves and earth, and built anew.

Many children build in this way, but more often than not as a social act, where they play the games of territory and society. For me it was important to be alone; solitude was a prerequisite to being openly and joyfully susceptible and responsive to the world of leaves, light, birdsong, flowers, flowing water. Most of the adult world spoke of such things as opportunities, and materials. To the young these materials are still celestial; for every child the garden is re-created. Then the occlusions begin. The mountain and the forest are sublime, but the valley soil raises richer crops. The perfect gift is no longer a single house but a house, or a mind, divided. Man finds he has two halves to his existence—leisure and occupation—and from these separate considerations he now looks upon the world. In leisure he remembers radiance; in labor he looks for results.

But in those early years I did not think about such things. I simply went out into the green world and made my house, a kind of cowl, or a dream, or a palace of grass.

3.

And now I am thinking of the poet Wordsworth, and the strange adventure that one night overtook him. When he was still a young boy, in love with summer and night, he went down to a lake, "borrowed" a rowboat, and rowed out upon the water. At first he felt himself embraced by pleasures: the moonlight, the sound of the oars in the calm water. Then, suddenly, a mountain peak nearby, with which he was familiar, or *felt* he was familiar, revealed, to his mind and eye, a horrifying flexibility. All crag and weight, it *perceived* him; it leaned down over the water; it seemed to pursue him. Of course he was terrified, and rowed hard, fleeing back across the water. But the experience led him, led his mind, from simple devotion of that beauty which is a harmony, a kindly ministry of thought, to nature's deeper and inexplicable greatness. The gleam and the tranquility of the natural world he loved always, and now he honored also the world's brawn and mystery, its machinations that lie beyond our understanding—that are not even nameable. What Wordsworth praised thereafter was more than the arrangement of concretions and vapors into appreciable and balanced landscapes; it was, also, the whirlwind. The beauty and strangeness of the world may fill the eyes with its cordial refreshment. Equally it may offer the heart a dish of terror. On one side is radiance; on another is the abyss.

4.

Wordsworth, though he did not think so on that summer evening, was a lucky boy. I, in my hut of leaves, was a lucky girl. Something touched, between us and the universe. It does not always happen. But if it does, we know forever where we live, no matter where we sleep, or eat our dinner, or sit at table and write words on paper.

And we might, in our lives, have many thresholds, many houses to walk out from and view the stars, or to turn and go back to for warmth and company. But the real one—the actual house not of beams and nails but of existence itself—is all of earth, with no door, no address separate from oceans or stars, or from pleasure or wretchedness either, or hope, or weakness, or greed.

How wonderful that the universe is beautiful in so many places and in so many ways. But also the universe is brisk and businesslike, and no doubt does not give its delicate landscapes or its thunderous displays of power, and perhaps perception, too, for our sakes or our improvement. Nevertheless, its intonations are our best tonics, if we would take them. For the universe is full of radiant suggestion. For whatever reason, the heart cannot separate the world's appearance and actions from morality and valor, and the power of every idea is intensified, if not actually created, by its expression in substance. Over and over in the butterfly we see the idea of transcendence. In the forest we see not the inert but the aspiring. In water that departs forever and forever returns, we experience eternity.

Swoon

In a corner of the stairwell of this rented house a most astonishing adventure is going on. It is only the household of a common spider,* a small, rather chaotic web half in shadow. Yet it burgeons with the ambition of a throne. She—for it is the female that is always in sight—has produced six egg sacs, and from three of them, so far, an uncountable number of progeny have spilled. "Spilled" is precisely the word, for the size and the motions of these newborns are so meager that they appear at first utterly lifeless, as though the hour of beginning had come and would not be deferred, and thrust them out, with or without their will, to cling in a dark skein in the tangled threads.

I am less precise about the timing of these events

---

*Probably *Parasteatoda tepidariorum*.

than I would like. While I was quick to notice the spider and her web, I was slow to write down the happenings as they occurred, a concordance I now wish I had. It was so casual at first, I was sure that something—probably a careless motion on my part—would demolish or tear the web and remove the spider from sight. But it did not happen.

I began to watch her in October, and it's fair to say that being a poor sleeper especially when away from home, I have watched her quite as much during the night as during the day.

Now it is early December.

I am extremely careful as I descend or ascend the stairs.

Perhaps when I pass by she senses my heft and shadow. But she floats on her strings and does not move. Nor, I think, would she flee easily from any intrusion. Her egg sacs, all of them, are hanging near her, in an archipel-ago, the oldest at the top and the newest at the bottom, and without question she is attached to them in some bond of cherishing. Often she lies with her face against the most recently constructed, touching it with her fore-most set of limbs. And why should she not be fond of it? She made it from the materials of her own body—deft and plump she circled and circled what was originally a small package, and caused it to grow larger as the thread flowed from her body. She wrapped and wrapped until, now, the sac sways with the others in the threads of the web, not round exactly, but like a Lilliputian gas balloon, pulled slightly along the vertical.

And still she fusses, pats it and circles it, as though coming to a judgment; then pats some more, or dozes, still touching it. Finally, she withdraws her sets of legs, curls them, almost as if in a swoon, or a death, and hangs, motionless, for a full half day. She seems to sleep.

The male spider comes and goes. Every third or fourth day I catch sight of him lurking at the edge of the web. What he eats I cannot guess, for the treasures of the web—which do not come, sometimes, for many days— are to all evidence for the female only. Whether she refuses to offer him a place at her table, or whether he has no need of it, I do not know. He is a dapper spider; being male and no spinner, he lacks the necessity of the pouch-like body in which to store the materials from which comes the bold and seemingly endless thread. He is therefore free to be of another nature altogether—small, and shy, and quick.

Twice while I have been watching, when the egg sacs have been in the unseeable process of pouring the tiny, billeted spiders forth, he has been in the web. Perhaps, like some male cats, and other mammals also, he will take this arrival with ill humor and feast on a few of his own progeny.

I do not know.

Whenever I see him poised there and lean closer to him, he steps briskly backward, is instantly enfolded into darkness and gone from sight.

It is five A.M.

Good fortune has struck the web like an avalanche. A cricket—not the black, flat-bodied, northern sort I am used to, but a paler variety, with a humped, shrimplike body and whiplike antennae and jumper's legs—has become enmeshed in the web.

This spider is not an orb weaver; that is, she does not build a net silken and organized and centered along a few strong cables. No, her web is a poor thing. It is flung forth, ungloriously, only a few inches above the cellar floor. What is visible is in a wild disorder. Nevertheless, it functions; it holds, now, the six egg cases and the cricket, which struggles in a sort of sling of webbing.

The spider now is never still. She descends to the cricket again and again, then hastens away and hangs a short distance above. Though it is almost impossible to see, a fine line follows her, jetting from her spinneret; as she moves, she is wrapping the cricket. Soon the threads thicken; the cricket is bound with visible threads at the ankles, which keep it from tearing loose with the strength of the huge back legs. How does the spider know what it knows? Little by little the cricket's long front limbs with their serrated edges, flung in an outward gesture from its body, are also being wrapped. Soon the cricket's efforts to free itself are only occasional—a few yawings toward push or pull—then it is motionless.

All this has taken an hour.

There has been nothing consumable in the web for more than a week, during which time the spider has made her sixth egg case and, presumably, before that, carried through some motions of romance with her consort, and produced the actual eggs. Her body during this week—I mean that dust-colored, sofa-button, bulbous part of her body so visible to our eyes—has shrunk to half its previous size.

Then, as I continued to watch, the spider began a curious and coordinated effort. She dropped to the cricket and with her foremost limbs, which are her longest, she touched its body. The response was an immediate lurching of cricket, also spider and web. Swiftly she turned—she was, in fret, beginning the motions of turning even as she reached forward—and then, even before the cricket reacted, with her hindmost pair of limbs she *kicked* it. She did this over and over—descending, touching and turning, kicking—each of her kicks targeting the cricket's stretched-out back limbs. She did this perhaps twenty times. With every blow the cricket swung, then rocked back to motionlessness, the only signs of life a small, continual motion of the jointed mouth, and a faint bubbling therefrom.

As I watched, the spider wrapped its thread again around the cricket's ankles. Then, with terrible and exact precision, she moved toward an indentation of flesh just at the elbow joint of the cricket's left front limb—and to this soft place she dipped her mouth. But, yet again, at this touch, the cricket lurched. So she retreated, and waited, and then again, with an undivertable aim, descended to that elbow where, finally, with no reaction from the cricket, she was able for perhaps three minutes to place her small face. There, as I imagine it, she began to infuse her flesh-dissolving venom into the channels of the cricket's body. Intermittently the cricket still moved, so this procedure even yet required some stopping and restarting, but it was clearly an unretractable operation. At length, in twenty minutes perhaps, the cricket lay utterly quiescent; and then the spider moved, with the most gentle and certain of motions, to the cricket's head, its bronze, visor-like face, and there, again surely and with no hesitation, the spider positioned her body, her mouth once more at some chosen juncture, near the throat, the spinal cord, the brain.

Now she might have been asleep as she lay, lover-like, alongside the cricket's body. Later—hours later—she moved down along its bronze chest, and there fed again. Slowly her shrunken body grew larger, then very large. And then it was night.

Early in the morning, the cricket was gone. As I learned from later examples, when the quiescent cricket was no more than a shell, she had cut it loose. It had dropped to the cellar floor, where any number of living crickets occasionally went leaping by. By any one of them it had been dragged away. Now the spider, engorged, was motionless. She slept with her limbs enfolded slightly—the same half clench of limbs one sees in the bodies of dead spiders—but this was the twilight rest, not the final one. This was the restoration, the interval, the sleep of the exhausted and the triumphant.

I have not yet described the mystery and enterprise for which she lives—the egg sacs and the young spiders. They emerge from their felt balloon and hang on threads near it: a fling, a nebula. Only by putting one's face very close, and waiting, and not breathing, can one actually see that the crowd is moving. It is motion not at all concerted or even definite, but it is motion, and that, compared with no movement at all, is of course everything. And it grows. Perhaps the spiders feel upon the tender hairs of their bodies the cool, damp cellar air, and it is a lure. They want more. They want to find out things. The tiny limbs stretch and shuffle.

Little by little, one or two, then a dozen, begin to drift into a wider constellation—toward the floor or the stair wall—spreading outward even as the universe is said to be spreading toward the next adventure and the next, endlessly.

In six or seven days after their birth, the little spiders are gone. And my attention passes from that opened and shrunken pod to the next below it, which is still secretly ripening, in which the many minuscule bodies are still packed tightly together, like a single thing.

How do they get out of the egg sac? Do they tear it with their fragile limbs? Do they chew it with their unimaginably tiny mouths?

I do not know.

Nor do I know where they all go, though I can imagine the dispersal of thousands into the jaws of the pale, leaping crickets. Certainly only a few of them survive, or we would be awash upon their rippling exertions.

Only once in this space of time, after the bursting of three of the six pods, did I see what was clearly a young spider; many times its original birth size and still no larger than a pencil's point, it was crawling steadily away through a last hem of the mother web.

This is the moment in an essay when the news culminates and, subtly or bluntly, the moral appears. It is a music to be played with the lightest fingers. All the questions that the spider's curious life made me ask, I know I can find answered in some book of knowledge, of which there are many. But the palace of knowledge is different from the palace of discovery, in which I am, truly, a Copernicus. *The world is not what I thought, but different, and more! I have seen it with my own eyes!*

But a spider? Even that?

Even that.

Our time in this rented house was coming to an end. For days I considered what to do with the heroine of this story and her enterprise, or if I should do anything at all. The owners of the house were to return soon; no reason to think they would not immediately sweep her away. And, in fact, we had ordered a housecleaning directly following our departure. Should I attempt to move her, therefore? And if so, to what place? To the dropping temperatures of the yard, where surely she could not last out the coming winter? To another basement corner? But would the crickets be there? Would the shy male spider find her? Could I move the egg sacs without harming them, and the web intact, to hold them?

Finally, I did nothing. I simply was not able to risk wrecking her world, and I could see no possible way I could move the whole kingdom. So I left her with the only thing I could—the certainty of a little more time. For our explicit and stern instructions to the cleaners were to scrub the house—but to stay out of this stairwell altogether.

Bird

"The light of the body is the eye."

(MATTHEW 6:22)

On a December morning, many years ago, I brought a young, injured black-backed gull home from the beach. It was, in fact, Christmas morning, as well as bitter cold, which may account for my act. Injured gulls are common; nature's maw receives them again implacably; almost never is a rescue justified by a return to health and freedom. And this gull was close to that deep maw; it made no protest when I picked it up, the eyes were half-shut, the body so starved it seemed to hold nothing but air.

A bathtub is a convenient and cool place in which to put an injured bird, and there this bird lay, on its side, through the rest of the day. But the next morning, its eyes were open and it sat, though clumsily, erect. It lifted its head and drank from a cup of water, little sips. It was a shattered elegance, grossly injured; the outer bone of one wing broken, the other wing injured as well. Our guess was that it had become hurt and unable to fly, and on the beach had been mauled by a dog or coyote. In the language of the day, it was bankrupt.

But the following morning it accepted food, a few small pieces of fresh cod. Food gave it strength and it rapidly became, in spite of its injuries, almost jaunty. The neck and breast muscles were strong; the eye, bright and clear. M. and I talked to it, it looked at us directly. It showed neither fear nor aggression, and we sensed quickly that it did not like to be alone.

We set up a site, with a padding of towels and paper towels, just inside a glass door that overlooks our deck and the harbor. It was apparent then that the gull was also leg-injured; it stood, but could not walk. In the first days one pink foot turned black and withered; later the remaining foot would do the same. When that happened we built up the perch to compensate, that he might still see outside. At the end of the day, when it grew dark, we turned him around to face the room, that he might be part of the evening circle.

He loved the light. In the morning when I came downstairs in the half-dark, he was eager for me to lift the shade and turn him around so he could begin looking. He would swing his head slowly from east to west, and back, and again, gazing slowly and deeply. During the colorful winter sunsets, the descent of the light, he also turned his attention entirely from us, and into the world.

To understand this, you must know that at other times he was greatly interested in us, and watched whatever we did with gorgeous curiosity. One morning I dropped next to him, by accident, a sheet of holiday wrapping paper, and I very soon saw him pecking at it. Diligently and persistently, he was trying to remove Santa Claus's hat from the Santa figure on the paper. After that we invented games; I drew pictures—of fish, of worms, of leggy spiders, of hot dogs—which he would pick at with a particularly gleeful intent. Since he was not hungry, his failure to lift the image seemed not to frustrate but to amuse him. We added feather-tossing, using crow feathers. I tossed by hand, he with his enormous, deft beak. We kept within his reach a bowl of sand and another of water, and began more nonsense—I would fling the water around with my finger, he, again, would follow with that spirited beak, dashing the water from the bowl, making it fly in all directions. His eyes sparkled. We gave him a stuffed toy—a lion as it happened—and he would peck the lion's red nose very gently, and lean against him while he slept.

And we had other moments of exhilaration and fun.

Every morning we filled the bathtub and he took boister-
ous baths, dipping his speckled head and beating the
water as well as he could, his shoulders shaking and his
wings partially opening. Then, on an island of towels, in
the morning sun, he would slowly and assiduously groom
himself. On a few windless days he sat on the deck
outside, a place safe from trouble and full of brightness. When we carried him there he would croak with
excitement.

But no matter how hard I try to tell this story, it's not
like it was. He was a small life but elegant, courteous,
patient, responsive, as well as very injured. And there is
this certainty about muscles; they need to be exercised.
And this was an enterprise in which he could no longer,
to any useful extent, engage. At the same time he was
gaining in attentiveness and eating more than suffi-
ciently, he was growing weaker. The wing wound had
dried, but the second foot had now begun to wither. He
shook his shoulders less and less during his bath. The
neck was still strong, the head lightly uplifted and
arched, quick and nimble. He was no less ready to play.
But, always, he was a little weaker. And so he was in an
impossible place. And we were more and more in a difficult place. How do I say it? We grew fond. We grew
into that perilous place: we grew fond.

We tried to kill him, with sleeping pills, but he only

slept for a long time, many hours, then woke with his usual brightness. We decided nature knows best and carried him back to the water and let him go, drifting, but he sank, so we waded out and got hold of him, all of us dripping wet as we carried him back inside.

January passed. As we entered February he ate voraciously, made a hundred messes on well-placed paper towels, or somewhere near them. By that time he knew the routines of the day, and expressed vigorous excitement toward the satisfaction of his anticipation. We had a storm from the southeast and I found along the shore a feast of soft-shelled clams; he ate until his eyes filled with sleep. The broken part of the wing hung now by a single tendon; we clipped it away. One withered foot literally fell from him, along with the first section of leg bone, so he was a one-winged, one-legged gull. But still patient, attentive.

And he had visitors. He liked to have his head touched, his feathers roughed up a little and then smoothed—something a two-legged gull can do for himself. He would sport with his water bowl. He would open the great beak for a feather, then fling it across the floor. He liked applause.

Was he in pain? Our own doctor, who came to see him, did not think so. Did we do right or wrong to lengthen his days? Even now we do not know. Sometimes he was restless. Then I would take him with me into the room where I write, and play music—Schubert, Mahler, Brahms. Soon he would become quiet, and, dipping his head, would retire into the private chamber of himself.

But the rough-and-tumble work of dying was going on, even in the quiet body. The middle of February passed. When I picked him up the muscles along the breast were so thin I feared for the tender skin lying across the crest of the bone. And still the eyes were full of the spices of amusement.

He was, of course, a piece of the sky. His eyes said so. This is not fact; this is the other part of knowing something, when there is no proof, but neither is there any way toward disbelief. Imagine lifting the lid from a jar and finding it filled not with darkness but with light. Bird was like that. Startling, elegant, alive.

But the day we knew must come did at last, and then the nonresponsiveness of his eyes was terrible. It was late February when I came downstairs, as usual, before dawn. Then returned upstairs, to M. The sweep and play of the morning was just beginning, its tender colors reaching everywhere. "The little gull has died," I said to M., as I lifted the shades to the morning light.

Owls

Upon the dunes and in the shaggy woodlands of the Province Lands, I have seen plenty of owls. Heard them at twilight and in the dark, and near dawn. Watched them, flying over Great Pond, flying over Rose Tasha's noisy barnyard, flying out of the open fretwork of the spire of the old Methodist church on Commercial Street, where the pigeons sleep, and disappear one by one. I have seen them in every part of the woods, favoring this or that acreage until the rabbits are scarce and they move to new hunting grounds, and then, in a few seasons, move back.

In January and February I walk in the woods and look for a large nest in a tall tree. In my mind's eye I see the great horned, the early nester, sitting upon her bulk of sticks, like an old woman on a raft.

I look in every part of the Province Lands that is

within my walking range. I look by Clapps Pond and Bennett Pond and Round Pond and Oak-Head Pond. I look along the riding trail that borders the landfill—in the old days a likely hunting ground and not one disdained by the owls or much else. I look in the woods close to the airport, so often have I flushed an owl from the pine trees there.

And I look in the woods around Pasture Pond, where, over a century ago, Mr. George Washington Ready, once the Provincetown town crier, saw the six-eyed sea serpent. He witnessed it, he said, emerging from the ocean and slithering across the dunes. Into Pasture Pond it descended, and sank from sight. Every winter I stare into the ice of the pond and think of it—still asleep, I suppose, in the clasp of the lily roots, for no one has ever seen it again.

And I search in the deeper woods, past fire roads and the bike trail, among the black oaks and the taller pines, in the silent blue afternoons, when the sand is still frozen and the snow falls slowly and aimlessly, and the whole world smells like water in an iron cup. And I see, on my way to the owl's nest, many marvelous things: the gray hives of the paper wasps, hidden in summer by the leaves but now apparent on the boughs; nests, including one of the Baltimore oriole, with fishline woven into it, so that it has in the wind a comet's tail of rippling white threads;

and pheasants, birds that were released into fall's russet fields but find themselves still alive at the far end of winter, and are glad of it, storming upward from the fields on their bright wings; and great blue herons, thin and melancholy; and deer, in their gray winter coats, bounding through the cold bogs; an owl in a tree with an unexpected face—a barred owl, seen once and once only.

Finally the earth grows softer, and the buds on the trees swell, and the afternoon becomes a wider room to roam in, as the sun moves back from the south and the light grows stronger. The bluebirds come back, and the robins, and the song sparrows, and great robust flocks of blackbirds; and in the fields blackberry hoops put on a soft plum color, a restitution; the ice on the ponds begins to thunder, and between the slices is seen the strokes of its breaking up, a stutter of dark lightning. And then the winter is over, and again I have not found the great horned owl's nest.

But the owls themselves are not hard to find, silent and on the wing, with their ear tufts flat against their heads as they fly and their huge wings alternately gliding and flapping as they maneuver through the trees. Athena's owl of wisdom and Merlin's companion, Archimedes, were screech owls surely, not this bird with the glassy gaze, restless on the bough, nothing but blood on its mind.

When the great horned is in the trees its razor-tipped toes rasp the limb; flakes of bark fall through the air and land on my shoulders while I look up at it and listen to the heavy, crisp, breathy snapping of its hooked beak. The screech owl I can imagine on my wrist, also the delicate saw-whet that flies like a big soft moth down by Great Pond. And I can imagine sitting quietly before that luminous wanderer the snowy owl, and learning, from the white gleam of its feathers, something about the arctic. But the great horned I can't imagine in any such proximity—if one of those should touch me, it would touch to the center of my life, and I must fall. They are the pure wild hunters of our world. They are swift and merciless upon the backs of rabbits, mice, voles, snakes, even skunks, even cats sitting in dusky yards, thinking peaceful thoughts. I have found the headless bodies of rabbits and blue jays, and known it was the great horned owl that did them in, taking the head only, for the owl has an insatiable craving for the taste of brains. I have walked with prudent caution down paths at twilight when the dogs were puppies. I know this bird. If it could, it would eat the whole world.

In the night, when the owl is less than exquisitely swift and perfect, the scream of the rabbit is terrible. But the scream of the owl, which is not of pain and hopelessness and the fear of being plucked out of the world, but of the sheer rollicking glory of the death-bringer, is more terrible still. When I hear it resounding through the woods, and then the five black pellets of its song dropping like stones into the air, I know I am standing at the edge of the mystery, in which terror is naturally and abundantly part of life, part of even the most becalmed, intelligent, sunny life—as, for example, my own. The world where the owl is endlessly hungry and endlessly on the hunt is the world in which I live too. There is only one world.

Sometimes, while I have stood listening to the owl's song drifting through the trees, when it is ten degrees above nothing—and life for any small creature is hard enough without *that*—I have found myself thinking of summer fields. Fields full of flowers—poppies or lupines. Or, here, fields where the roses hook into the dunes, and their increase is manyfold. All summer they are red and pink and white tents of softness and nectar, which wafts and hangs everywhere—a sweetness so palpable and excessive that, before it, I'm struck, I'm taken, I'm conquered; I'm washed into it, as though it was a river, full of dreaming and idleness—I drop to the sand, I can't move; I am restless no more; I am replete, supine, finished, filled to the last edges with an immobilizing happiness. And is this not also terrible? Is this not also frightening?

Are the roses not also—even as the owl is—excessive? Each flower is small and lovely, but in their sheer and silent abundance the roses become an immutable force, as though the work of the wild roses was to make sure that all of us who come wandering over the sand may be, for a while, struck to the heart and saturated with a simple joy. Let the mind be teased by such *stretches* of the imagination, by such balance. Now I am cringing at the very sound of the owl's dark wings opening over my head—not long ago I could do nothing but lounge on the sand and stare into the cities of the roses.

I have two feathers from the big owl. One I found near Round Pond; the other, on another day, fell as I watched the bird rise from one tree and flap into another. As the owl rose, some crows caught sight of it, and so began another scrimmage in their long battle. The owl wants to sleep, but the crows pursue it and when it settles a second time the crows—now a dozen—gather around and above it, and scream into its face, with open beaks and wagging tongues. They come dangerously close to its feet, which are huge and quick. The caught crow is a dead crow. But it is not in the nature of crows to hide or cower—it is in their nature to gather and to screech and to gamble in the very tree where death stares at them with molten eyes. What fun, to aggravate the old bomber! What joy, to swipe at the tawny feathers even as the bird puffs and hulks and hisses.

But finally the owl rises from the trees altogether and climbs and floats away, over two or three hills, and the crows go off to some other merriment.

And I walk on, over the shoulder of summer and down across the red-dappled fall; and, when it's late winter again, out through the far woodlands of the Province Lands, maybe another few hundred miles, looking for the owl's nest, yes, of course, and looking at everything else along the way.

Two Short Ones

1. Who Cometh Here?

Years after I wrote a joke poem about a black bear being sighted in our neighboring town, Truro, one adventurer did actually come, crossing Massachusetts, swimming the channel, striding the length of the Cape to the end of it. One can imagine him staring out at the water—waves to the coast of Portugal—before he sighed and turned back.

He did no harm, was seen almost rubbing up against the Provincetown Town Hall, striding the edge of Route 6, and finally (who can blame him?) invading a beehive in the town of Wellfleet. There he was captured, tranquilized, tagged, and trucked back to where, by the rangers' best guess, he had begun his journey.

Most residents on the Cape were relieved. But a few, myself among them, had other thoughts.

The truth is, he was probably looking for a partner, and he certainly wasn't the first of our sort—though possibly the first of his—to visit Provincetown for the same purpose. In any case, he didn't come to stir up the government, or open another café or—heaven forbid—a fast-food restaurant, or mouth off opinions about gay, antigay, or what he thought of the artists, or write end-less complaining letters to the town paper.

Yes, I suppose he must have poached a few fish. But on the other hand think what a valuable resident he might have become, had he been willing to join in our charitable events (a hundred dollars for a chance to go dancing with Provincetown's very own bear!). Also, with his preference for camping out he certainly wouldn't have left behind the necessities and amenities in obvious distress.

Dear Bear, it's no use, the world is like that. So stay where you are, and live long. Someday maybe we'll wise up and remember what you were: hopeless ambassador of a world that returns now only in poets' dreams.

2. Ropes

In the old days dogs in our town roamed freely. But the old ways changed.

One morning a puppy arrived in our yard with a length of rope hanging from his collar. He played with our dogs; eventually he vanished. But the next morning he showed up again, with a different rope attached. This happened for a number of days—he appeared, he was playful and friendly, and always accompanied by a chewed-through rope.

Just at that time we were moving to another house, which we finished doing all in one evening. A day or so later, on a hunch, I drove back to the old house and found him lying in the grass by our door. I put him in the car and showed him where our new house was. "Do your best," I said.

He stayed around for a while, then was gone. But there he was the next morning at the new house. Rope dangling. Later that day his owner appeared—with his papers from the Bideawee home, and a leash. "His name is Sammy," she said. "And he's yours."

As Sammy grew older he began to roam around

the town and, as a result, began to be caught by the dog officer. Eventually, of course, we were summoned to court, which, we learned quickly, was not a place in which to argue. We were told to build a fence. Which we did.

But it turned out that Sammy could not only chew through ropes, he could also climb fences. So his roaming continued.

But except for the dog officer, Sammy never got into trouble; he made friends. He wouldn't fight with other dogs, he just seemed to stay awhile in someone's yard and, if possible, to say hello to the owners. People began to call us to come and get him before the dog officer saw him. Some took him into their houses to hide him from the law. Once a woman on the other end of town called; when I got there she said, "Can you wait just a few minutes? I'm making him some scrambled eggs."

I could tell many more stories about Sammy—they're endless. But I'll just tell you the unexpected, joyful conclusion. The dog officer resigned! And the next officer was a different sort; he too remembered and missed the old days. So when he found Sammy he would simply call him into his truck and drive him home. In this way, he lived a long and happy life, with many friends.

This is Sammy's story. But I also think there are

one or two poems in it somewhere. Maybe it's what life was like in this dear town years ago, and how a lot of us miss it.

Or maybe it's about the wonderful things that may happen if you break the ropes that are holding you.

Winter Hours

In the winter I am writing about, there was much darkness. Darkness of nature, darkness of event, darkness of
the spirit. The sprawling darkness of *not knowing*. We
speak of the light of reason. I would speak here of the
darkness of the world, and the light of _____. But I
don't know what to call it. Maybe hope. Maybe faith,
but not a shaped faith—only, say, a gesture, or a con-
tinuum of gestures. But probably it is closer to hope, that
is more active, and far messier than faith must be. Faith,
as I imagine it, is tensile, and cool, and has no need of
words. Hope, I know, is a fighter and a screamer.

The house is hard cold. Winter walks up and down the
town swinging his censer, but no smoke or sweetness
comes from it, only the sour, metallic frankness of salt

and snow. I dress in the dark and hurry out. The sleepy dogs walk with me a few strides, then they disappear. The water slaps crisply upon the cold-firmed sand. I listen intently, as though it is a language the ocean is speaking. There are no stars, nor a moon. Still I can tell that the tide is rising, as it speaks singingly, and I can see a little from the street lamps and from the amber lights along the wharf. The water tosses its black laces and flaunts, streaked with the finest rain. Now and again the dogs come back, their happy feet dashing the sand. Before we reach the seawall again, and cross the yard, it is no longer night. We stand by the door of the house. We stand upon the thin blue peninsula that leads to the sharp white day. A small black cat bounds from under the rosebushes; the dogs bark joyfully.

This is the beginning of every day.

I have never been to Rome. I have never been to Paris, or Greece, or Sweden. I went once to England, so long ago it seems like the Middle Ages. M. and I went once to the Far East, Japan and Malaysia and New Zealand and Indonesia, and I am glad I saw the Southern Cross, but I have not forgotten how it felt to think I was going to fall off the planet. I am not a traveler. Not of that sort.

I do know the way to the grocery store, and I can get that far. The simples of our lives: bread, fruit, vegetables. In the big store. The old small stores, with which I was long familiar, are gone. Though there are new ones, to suit new purposes. Previously there were small shops because it was a small town. Now there are small shops because the tourists want to think they are still in that little town, which has vanished. It is good business now to appear antiquated, with narrow aisles and quaintly labeled jars.

From the oldest resource of all, the sea, still comes food, occasionally, by hook or by chance. One morning I find three fish on the beach as fresh as young celery—cod, each of them a little over a foot long. I bring them home. The largest of the three has been gaffed, so it is probable the fish came from the wharf, having escaped some packing crate or boat. The three fish have made their landfall close together, which bespeaks the purposeful motions of the tide as it laps toward shore. The fish are exquisite, with torpedo-shaped bodies, dark speckles under a sea-green glaze, hard heads with a fleshy jaw appendage, large eyes. They have many small cutting teeth, but by no means like those of the more aggressive bluefish. Neither is there any sudden place along the spine where the hand, unaware, could be badly tapped or torn, as there is on the body of the bluefish.

I clean the fish and call M. to come and see the insides of the last one, before I scoop the ship of its body to a smooth emptiness. The many shapes and shades of pink are astounding—the heart, the frillery and drapery of the lungs, the swim bladder, the large liver. The tongue in the wide mouth, pale and fat, is like the tongue of a newborn pug.

In fact, there is something called tongues and cheeks in the fish shops. Now I see on each head two areas, the size of half-dollars, where I might have lifted out a fine plug of flesh, and gone a-chowdering. Instead I take the heads, spines, etc., out to the beach, in a blue pail, and dump them on an influx of sand. A few gulls in the distance cry out and are there almost on one wing-pull. They make quick work of all of it, in the pink-tipped light.

The fish are delicious.

For years when the tide was high I went, early or late, to another part of this world, which is mostly pinewoods. What you imagine when I say "pine" might not be our variety, which is also called pitch pine, or scrub pine. It is a modest tree, twisty and aromatic. It can live in the face of the sea wind, giving up chances for girth and height, perhaps, for valuable elasticity. There are black oaks also, and tupelos that tend to set down roots in the dampness along the edges of the ponds.

Through these woods I have walked thousands of times. For many years I felt more at home here than anywhere else, including our own house. Stepping out into the world, into the grass, onto the path, was always a kind of relief. I was not escaping anything. I was returning to the arena of delight. I was stepping across some border. I don't mean just that the world changed on the other side of the border, but that I did too. Eventually I began to appreciate—I don't say this lightly—that the great black oaks knew me. I don't mean they knew me as myself and not another—that kind of individualism was not in the air—but that they recognized and responded to my presence, and to my mood. They began to offer, or I began to feel them offer, their serene greeting. It was like a quick change of temperature, a warm and comfortable flush, faint yet palpable, as I walked toward them and beneath their outflowing branches.

In the pinewoods is where the owl floats, and where the white egret paces, in summer, like a winged snake, in the flashing shallows. Here is where two deer approached me one morning, in an unforgettable sweetness, their faces like light-brown flowers, their eyes kindred and full of curiosity. The mouth of one of them, and its vibrant tongue, licked my hand. This is where the coyotes appeared, one season, and followed me, bold beyond belief, and nimble—lean ferocities just held in check. This is where, once, I heard suddenly a powerful beating of wings, a feisty rhythm, a pomp of sound, within it a thrust then a slight uptake. The wings of angels might sound so, who are after all not mild but militant, and cross the skies on important missions. Then, just above the trees, their feet trailing and their eyes blazing, two swans flew by.

There is a place in the woods where the vanishing bodies of our dogs, our dogs of the past, lie in the sweet-smelling earth. How they ran through these woods! Too late, world, to deny them their lives of motion, of burly happiness. After Luke died, I crossed and recrossed the Province Lands, wherever we had been, and wherever I found her paw-prints in the sand I dragged branches and leaves and slabs of bark over them, so they would last, would keep from the wind a long time. Then, overnight, after maybe three weeks, in a dazzling, rearranging rain, they were gone.

When I came to a teachable age, I was, as most youngsters are, directed toward the acquisition of knowledge, meaning not so much ideas but demonstrated facts. Education as I knew it was made up of such a preestablished collection of certainties.

Knowledge has entertained me and it has shaped me and it has failed me. Something in me still starves. In what is probably the most serious inquiry of my life, I have begun to look past reason, past the provable, in other directions. Now I think there is only one subject worth my attention and that is the precognition of the spiritual side of the world and, within this recognition, the condition of my own spiritual state. I am not talking about having faith necessarily, although one hopes to. What I mean by spirituality is not theology, but attitude. Such interest nourishes me beyond the finest compendium of facts. In my mind now, in any comparison of demonstrated truths and unproven but vivid intuitions, the truths lose.

I would therefore write a kind of elemental poetry that doesn't just avoid indoors but doesn't even *see* the doors that lead inward—to laboratories, to textbooks, to knowledge. I would not talk about the wind, and the oak tree, and the leaf on the oak tree, but on their behalf. I would talk about the owl and the thunderworm and the daffodil and the red-spotted newt as a company of spirits, as well as bodies. I would say that the fox stepping out over the snow has nerves as fine as mine, and a better courage. I would write praise poems that might serve as comforts, reminders, or even cautions if needed, to wayward minds and unawakened hearts.

I would say that there exist a thousand unbreakable links between each of us and everything else, and that our dignity and our chances are one. The farthest star and the mud at our feet are a family; and there is no decency or sense in honoring one thing, or a few things, and then closing the list. The pine tree, the leopard, the Platte River, and ourselves—we are at risk together, or we are on our way to a sustainable world together. We are each other's destiny.

I could not be a poet without the natural world. Someone else could. But not me. For me the door to the woods is the door to the temple.

Building the House

1.

I know a young man who can build almost anything—a boat, a fence, kitchen cabinets, a table, a barn, a house. And so serenely, and in so assured and right a manner, that it is joy to watch him. All the same, what he seems to care for best—what he seems positively to desire—is the hour of interruption, of hammerless quiet, in which he will sit and write down poems or stories that have come into his mind with clambering and colorful force. Truly he is not very good at the puzzle of words—not nearly as good as he is with the mallet and the measuring tape—but this in no way lessens his pleasure. Moreover, he is in no hurry. Everything he learned, he learned at a careful pace—will not the use of words come easier at last, though he begin at the slowest trot? Also, in these intervals, he is happy. In building things, he is his familiar self, which he does not overvalue. But in the act of writing he is a grander man, a surprise to us, and even more to himself. He is beyond what he believed himself to be.

I understand his pleasure. I also know the enclosure of my skills, and am no less pert than he when some flow takes me over the edge of it. Usually, as it happens, this is toward the work in which he is so capable. There appears in my mind a form; I imagine it from boards of a certain breadth and length, and nails, and all in cheerful response to some need I have or think I have, aligned with a space I see as opportunistic. I would not pry my own tooth, or cobble my own shoes, but I deliberate unfazed the niceties of woodworking—nothing, all my life, has checked me. At my side at this moment is a small table with one leg turned in slightly. For I have never at all built anything perfectly, or even very well, in spite of the pleasure such labor gives me. Nor am I done yet, though time has brought obstacles and spread them before me—a stiffness of the fingers, a refusal of the eyes to switch easily from near to far, or rather from far to near, and thus to follow the aim of the hammer toward the nail head, which yearly grows smaller, and smaller.

Once, in fact, I built a house. It was a minuscule house, a one-room, one-floored affair set in the ivies and vincas of the backyard, and made almost entirely of salvaged materials. Still, it had a door. And four windows. And, miraculously, a peaked roof, so I could stand easily inside, and walk around. After it was done, and a door hung, I strung a line from the house so that I could set a lamp upon the built-in table, under one of the windows. Across the yard, in the evening with the lamplight shining outward, it looked very sweet, and it gave me much satisfaction. It seemed a thing of great accomplishment, as indeed, for me, it was. It was the house I had built. There would be no other.

The labor of writing poems, of working with thought and emotion in the encasement (or is it the wings?) of language, is strange to nature, for we are first of all creatures of motion. Only secondly—only oddly, and not naturally, at moments of contemplation, joy, grief, prayer, or terror—are we found, while awake, in the posture of deliberate or hapless inaction. But such is the posture of the poet, poor laborer. The dancer dances, the painter dips and lifts and lays on the oils, the composer reaches at least across the octaves. The poet sits. The architect draws and measures, and travels to the quarry to tramp among the gleaming stones. The poet sits, or, if it is a fluid moment, he scribbles some words upon the page. The body, under this pressure of nonexisting, begins to draw up like a muscle, and complain. An unsolvable disharmony of such work—the mind so

MARY OLIVER

hotly fired and the body so long quiescent—will come sooner or later to revolution, will demand action! For many years, in a place I called Blackwater Woods, I wrote while I walked. That motion, hardly more than a dreamy sauntering, worked for me; it kept my body happy while I scribbled. But sometimes it wasn't at all enough. I wanted to build, in the other way, with the teeth of the saw, and the explosions of the hammer, and the little shrieks of the screws winding down into their perfect nests.

2.

I began the house when I returned one spring after a year of teaching in a midwestern city. I had been, for months, responsible, sedate, thoughtful, and, for most of my daylight hours, indoors. I was sick for activity. And so, instead of lingering on the porch with my arrangement of tools, banging and punching together some simple and useful thing—another bookshelf, another table—I began the house.

When anything is built in our town, it is more importantly a foundation than a structure. Nothing—be it ugly, nonconforming, in violation of bylaws or neighbors' rights—nothing, once up, has ever been torn down.

And almost nothing exists as it was originally constructed. On our narrow strip of land we are a build-up, add-on society. My house today, crooked as it is, stands. It has an undeniable value: it exists. It may therefore be enlarged eventually, even unto rentable proportions. The present owners of the property would not dream of discarding it. I can see from the road, they have given it a new roof and straightened out some doubtful portions of the peaked section. To one end of the peak, they have attached a metal rod that holds, in the air above the house, a statue of a heron, in the attitude of easy flight. My little house, looking upward, must be astonished.

The tools I used in my building of the house, and in all my labor of this sort, were a motley assortment of hand tools: hammer, tack hammer, drivers of screws, rasps, planes, saws small-toothed and rip, pliers, wrenches, awls. They had once belonged to my grandfather, and some of them to my great-grandfather, who was a carpenter of quality, and used the finer title "cabinetmaker." This man I know only from photographs and an odd story or two: for example, he built his own coffin, of walnut, and left it, to be ready when needed, with the town mortician. Eventually, like the tiniest of houses, and with his body inside, it was consumed by flame.

These tools, though so closely mine, were not made therefore easy for me to use. I was, frankly, accident-prone; while I was making anything my hands and shins and elbows, if not other parts of my body, were streaked with dirt and nicks. Gusto, not finesse, was my trademark here. And often enough, with these tools, I would come to a place where I could not wrest some necessary motion from my own wrists, or lift, or cut through. Then I would have to wait, in frustration, for a friend or acquaintance, or even a stranger—male, and stronger than I—to come along, and I would simply ask for help to get past that instant, that twist of the screw. Provincetown men, though they may seem rough to the unknowing, are as delicious and courteous as men are made. "Sure, darling," the plumber would say, or the neighbor passing by, or the fisherman stepping over from his yard, and he would help me, and would make a small thing of it.

3.

Whatever a house is to the heart and body of man—refuge, comfort, luxury—surely it is as much or more to the spirit. Think how often our dreams take place inside the houses of our imaginations! Sometimes these are fearful, gloomy, enclosed places. At other times they are bright and have many windows and are surrounded by gardens combed and invitational, or unpathed and wild. Surely such houses appearing in our sleep-work represent the state of the soul, or, if you prefer it, the state of the mind. Real estate, in any case, is not the issue of dreams. The condition of our true and private self is what dreams are about. If you rise refreshed from a dream—a night's settlement inside some house that has filled you with pleasure—you are doing okay. If you wake to the memory of squeezing confinement, rooms without air or light, a door difficult or impossible to open, a troubling disorganization or even wreckage inside, you are in trouble—with yourself. There are (dream) houses that pin themselves upon the windy porches of mountains, that open their own windows and summon in flocks of wild and colorful birds—and there are houses that hunker upon narrow ice floes adrift upon endless, dark waters; houses that creak, houses that sing; houses that will say nothing at all to you though you beg and plead all night for some answer to your vexing questions.

As such houses in dreams are mirrors of the mind or the soul, so an actual house, such as I began to build, is at least a little of that inner state made manifest. Jung, in a difficult time, slowly built a stone garden and a stone tower. Thoreau's house at Walden Pond, ten feet by fifteen feet under the tall, arrowy pines, was surely a dream-shape come to life. For anyone, stepping away from actions where one knows one's measure is good. It shakes away an excess of seriousness. Building my house, or anything else, I always felt myself becoming, in an almost devotional sense, passive, and willing to play. Play is never far from the impress of the creative drive, never far from the happiness of discovery. Building my house, I was joyous all day long.

The material issue of a house, however, is a matter not so much of imagination and spirit as it is of particular, joinable, weighty substance—it is brick and wood, it is foundation and beam, sash and sill; it is threshold and door and the latch upon the door. In the seventies and the eighties, in this part of the world if not everywhere, there was an ongoing, monstrous binge of building, or tearing back and rebuilding—and carting away of old materials to the (then-titled) dump. Which, in those days, was a lively and even social place. Work crews made a continual effort toward bulldozing the droppings from the trucks into some sort of order, shoving at least a dozen categories of broken and forsaken materials, along with reusable materials, into separate areas. Gulls, in flocks like low white clouds, screamed and rippled over the heaps of lumber, looking for garbage that was also dumped, and often in no particular area. Motels, redecorating, would bring three hundred mattresses in the morning, three hundred desks in the afternoon. Treasures, of course, were abundantly sought and found. And good wood—useful wood—wood it was a sin to bury, not to use again. The price of lumber had not yet skyrocketed, so even new lumber lay seamed in with the old, the price passed on to the customer. Cutoffs, and lengths. Pine, fir, oak flooring, shingles of red and white cedar, ply, cherry trim, also tar paper and insulation, screen doors new and old, and stovepipe old and new, and bricks, and, more than once, some power tools left carelessly, I suppose, in a truck bed, under the heaps of trash. This is where I went for my materials, along with others, men and women both, who simply roved, attentively, through all the mess until they found what they needed, or felt they would, someday, use. Clothes, furniture, old dolls, old high chairs, bikes; once a child's metal bank in the shape of a dog, very old; once a set of copper-bottomed cookware still in its original cartons; once a bag of old Christmas cards swept from the house of a man who had died only a month or so earlier, in almost every one of them a dollar bill.

Here I found everything I needed, including nails from half-full boxes spilled into the sand. All I lacked—only because I lacked the patience to wait until it came along—was one of the ridge beams; this I bought at the local lumber company and paid cash for; thus the entire house cost me $3.58.

Oh, the intimidating and beautiful hardwoods! No more could I cut across the cherry or walnut or the oak than across stone! It was pine I looked for, with its tawny pattern of rings, its crisp knots, its willingness to be broken, cut, split, and its fragrance that never reached the air but made the heart gasp with its sweetness. Plywood I had no love of, though I took it when found and used it when I could, knowing it was no real thing, and alien to the weather, and apt to parch and swell, or buckle, or rot. Still, I used it. My little house was a patchwork. It was organic as a garden. It was free of any promise of exact inches, though at last it achieved a fair if not a strict linearity. On its foundation of old railroad ties, its framing of old wood, old ply, its sheets of tar paper, its rows of pale shingles, it stood up. Stemming together everything with sixpenny nails, eightpenny nails, spikes, screws, I was involved, frustrated, devoted, resolved, nicked and scraped, and delighted. The work went slowly. The roof went on, was shingled with red cedar. I was a poet, but I was away for a while from the loom of thought and formal language; I was playing. I was whimsical, absorbed, happy. Let me always be who I am, and then some.

When my house was finished, my friend Stanley Kunitz gave me a yellow door, discarded from his house at the other end of town. Inside, I tacked up a van Gogh landscape, a Blake poem, a photograph of Mahler, a picture M. had made with colored chalk. Some birds' nests hung in the corners. I lit the lamp. I was done.

4.

There is something you can tell people over and over, and with feeling and eloquence, and still never say it well enough for it to be more than news from abroad—people have no readiness for it, no empathy. It is the news of personal aging—of climbing, and knowing it, to some unrepeatable pitch and coming forth on the other side, which is pleasant still but which is, unarguably, different—which is the beginning of descent. It is the news that no one is singular, that no argument will change the course, that one's time is more gone than not, and what is left waits to be spent gracefully and attentively, if not quite so actively. The plumbers in town now are the sons of our old plumber. I cut some pine boards for some part of an hour, and I am tired. A year or so ago, hammering, I hit my thumb, directly and with force, and lost the nail for a half year. I was recently given a power drill, which also sets and removes screws. It could be a small cannon, so apprehensive am I of its fierce and quick power. When I handle it well (which to begin with means that I aim it correctly), difficult tasks are made easy. But when I do not, I hold an angry weasel in my hand.

I hardly used the little house—it became a place to store garden tools, boxes of this or that. Did I write one poem there? Yes, I did, and a few more. But its purpose never was to be shelter for thought. I built it *to build it*, stepped out over the threshold, and was gone.

I don't think I am old yet, or done with growing. But my perspective has altered—I am less hungry for the busyness of the body, more interested in the tricks of the mind. I am gaining, also, a new affection for wood that is useless, that has been tossed out, that merely exists, quietly, wherever it has ended up. Planks on the beach rippled and salt-soaked. Pieces of piling, full of the tunnels of shipworm. In the woods, fallen branches of oak, of maple, of the dear, wind-worn pines. They lie on the ground and do nothing. They are travelers on the way to oblivion.

The young man now—that carpenter we began with—places his notebook carefully beside him and rises and, as though he had just come back from some great distance, looks around. There are his tools, there is the wood; there is his unfinished task, to which, once more, he turns his attention. But life is no narrow business. On any afternoon he may hear and follow this same rhapsody, turning from his usual labor, swimming away into the pleasures, the current of language. More power to him!

For myself, I have passed him by and have gone into the woods. Near the path, one of the tall maples has fallen. It is early spring, so the crimped maroon flowers are just emerging. Here and there slabs of the bark have exploded away in the impact of its landing. But, mostly, it lies as it stood, though not such a net for the wind as it was. What is it now? What does it signify? Not Indolence, surely, but something, all the same, that balances with Ambition.

Call it Rest. I sit on one of the branches. My idleness suits me. I am content. I have built my house. The blue butterflies, called azures, twinkle up from the secret place where they have been waiting. In their small blue dresses they float among the branches, they come close to me, one rests for a moment on my wrist. They do not recognize me as anything very different from this enfoldment of leaves, this wind-roarer, this wooden palace lying down, now, upon the earth, like anything heavy, and happy, and full of sunlight, and half asleep.

SECTION FIVE

Provincetown

Give me a fish, I eat for a day:
teach me to fish, I eat for a lifetime.

FISHERMAN'S MOTTO

Now let my fingers and pencils and my beloved old machine with its letters and numbers fly over the sweet harbor and gaze instead into the town itself. A tiny town as towns and cities are now, but to me it held a perfect sufficiency. Front Street and Back Street. Of course they had other names, but this is town talk. One traffic light, one doctor, one drugstore. A scattering of restaurants, saloons. And the boatyards.

Most of the town lived for its fishing, a rough trade taken on, for the fish then were plenty. Many of the men were from Portugal, the islands. Not all of course, but their hardiness was noticeable. Men, and boys in small boats that scarcely ever carried emergency gear for the men. Which meant at times the loss of both, the boat and its crew. When a boat did not return there was grieving in more than one house. Still, the next morning the boats went out, without their brothers. It felt close to nobility.

A memory: hauling the net up to the surface of the water and onto the deck was not easy work; the men had to be strong, quick, and accurate. In the morning sun, a few of the old men, retired now, would often gather together on the bench in front of the New York Store. Not one of them had all ten fingers.

Speaking of the net, which sank deeply and broadly, many a curiosity might appear along with the catch. Once, a human leg bone. Certainly in these days it would have been taken to the police station, not so in the time I am talking of, but instead it was carried to the priest at the Catholic church. Where because of an old leg wound from the war, the owner of this piece of body was identified. Missing is only missing to insurance companies, but now the insurance would be paid, if the family had such. A blessing to a whole family.

The town was full of nicknames—a few I remember: Moon, Iron Man, Jimmy Peek (in remembrance of his grandfather, who, it is said, peeked a great deal). And then there was Flyer, owner of the boatyard. One winter, already of a great age, his shoulders stiffened into use-lessness. He filled two pails with sand and water and carried them everywhere he went, the entire winter. By spring his shoulders were fine. You do not meet such people everywhere.

I don't mean to slight the women of the town. Visiting a Portuguese house often deeply snuggled among flowers, it took no more than three minutes from my knock before I would find myself sitting in front of a bowl of steaming, delicious Portuguese soup and adding my own voice to the family chatter.

Provincetown has what we called Mediterranean light, which for years had brought artists to set up their easels on the shore, on the dunes, on street corners, or perhaps in their own houses. Writers came as well. No occupation was considered elite. Provincetown became the place to come not only for the light but for the friendliness that sustained all of us, or so it seemed. I meet the plumber in the hardware store, "How's your work going?" he would say. Pretty good, I'd answer, and how about you? "Pretty well," he would say. And we would both ramble off smiling, feeling the sweetness of it.

And then the terrible change began. The great rafts of fish began to diminish. The satisfaction of a day's work also began to vanish. Overfishing, climate change, and little boats that were growing older every year were the causes. In other towns, larger boats were built to travel farther out to sea, something the Provincetown fleet could not do.

A town cannot live on dreams. The change was slow but harsh. The young men and women, boys and girls left to find work and to build another life. And the town became, not all at once but steadily, a town of pleasure. People swarmed in on weekends, and they still do. And it will no doubt go on. And there is no blame in this. The town had to find another way to live.

The tourist business was in. Late into the night the bands played. Closing hours changed, became later. There were weekend people and people who could afford a longer stay or buy a summer home. At the same time, I must say that many of the changes were important. A home for young artists and painters was established as well as a scientific center for the study of our coastal waters. But generally it became just, well, different. One could say it fast became a place to visit or live for a while, and to spend money. Not so much in which to live a life. To dance and make noise, though

I do not mean to criticize all frolic. It was just, well, different.

I don't know if I am heading toward heaven or that other, dark place, but I know I have already lived in heaven for fifty years. Thank you, Provincetown.

ACKNOWLEDGMENTS

"Who Cometh Here?" was first published in *Appalachia Journal*.

Grateful acknowledgment is made for permission to reprint the following works:

"Upstream" from *Blue Iris: Poems and Essays* by Mary Oliver. Copyright © 2004 by Mary Oliver. Reprinted by permission of Beacon Press.

"Sister Turtle," "Building the House," "Winter Hours, "The Bright Eyes of Eleonora: Poe's Dream of Recapturing the Impossible," "Swoon," and "Some Thoughts on Whitman" from *Winter Hours: Prose, Prose Poems and Poems* by Mary Oliver. Copyright © 1999 by Mary Oliver. Reprinted by permission of Houghton Mifflin Harcourt Publishing Company. All rights reserved.

"Bird" from *Owls and Other Fantasies: Poems and Essays* by Mary Oliver. Copyright © 2003 by Mary Oliver. Reprinted by permission of Beacon Press.

ACKNOWLEDGMENTS

"Wordsworth's Mountain" from *Long Life: Essays and Other Writings* by Mary Oliver, copyright © 2004 by Mary Oliver. Reprinted by permission of Da Capo Press, an imprint of Perseus Books, a division of PBG Publishing, LLC, a subsidiary of Hachette Book Group, Inc.

"My Friend Walt Whitman," "Staying Alive," "Owls," "The Ponds," "Of Power and Time," and "Blue Pastures" from *Blue Pastures* by Mary Oliver. Copyright © 1995 by Mary Oliver. Reprinted by permission of Houghton Mifflin Harcourt Publishing Company. All rights reserved.

"Ropes" from *Dog Songs* by Mary Oliver (Penguin Press). Copyright © 2013 by Mary Oliver. Used by permission of Charlotte Sheedy Literary Agency.

"Emerson: An Introduction" by Mary Oliver, copyright © 2000 by Mary Oliver; from *The Essential Writings of Ralph Waldo Emerson* by Ralph Waldo Emerson, edited by Brooks Atkinson. Used by permission of Modern Library, an imprint of Random House, a division of Penguin Random House LLC. All rights reserved.